The TRUST of LEADERSHIP

Six Virtues of Trustworthy Leaders

-by-

Gregg T. Johnson

Global Leadership Training
2015

The Trust of Leadership

COPYRIGHT © 2015
©Gregg T. Johnson

All rights reserved. No part of this book may be reproduced, stored in a retrieval system, or transmitted in any form or by any means—electronic, mechanical, photocopy, recording, or any other—except for brief quotations in printed reviews, without the prior permission of Gregg T. Johnson.

All scripture quotations are taken from
The Holy Bible, New King James Version
Copyright © 1982 by Thomas Nelson, Inc.

Front Cover Picture:
Segovia Aqueduct
Sjoerd van der Wal Photography ©Sjo
Licensed by Getty Images (US), Inc.
via ww.iStockphoto.com

Special thanks to
Janet Spinelli-Dunn
For proofreading and editing

ISBN 978-0-9741036-5-5

First Printing: 2015

Global Leadership Training
The Mission Church
4101 Rt. 52
Holmes NY 12531, USA

Printed in the United States by Morris Publishing®
3212 East Highway 30
Kearney, NE 68847
1-800-650-7888

TABLE OF CONTENTS

Foreword *Dr. D.P. Durst, D. Min.*	4
Introduction	7
Accountability	15
Transparency	31
Reportability	39
Fiduciarity	55
Humility	71
Collegiality	87
A Final Word	103
Endnotes	106
About the Author	109

FOREWORD

Leadership ...is an everyday thing.
Lebron James

Leadership *is* an everyday thing. John Maxwell said, "Everything rises and falls on leadership." Leadership is a gift, a skill and an essential element of every organization, ministry or public institution that intends to have a positive impact on society. In *The Trust of Leadership,* Gregg Johnson describes the leadership qualities of accountability, openness, financial integrity, relationship and humility. Johnson is well qualified to address these topics, the everyday qualities of leadership.

As the founder and president of Global Leadership Training, Johnson has traveled the world training and inspiring government, business and church leaders in the art of leadership. Presidents, judiciary, government workers, corporate officers, pastors and denominational leaders have benefitted from the principles of leadership—integrity, ethics, character and accountability—that Johnson addresses in his six leadership books. His underlying emphasis on servant leadership mirrors that so initially defined by John Greenleaf in his book *The Servant as Leader.*

Gregg Johnson not only writes and teaches leadership principles, he lives them out on a daily basis. As a pastor he models great leadership before his congregation and the leaders of The Mission Church. Rarely have I seen church leaders as devoted to their pastor and committed to his calling to raise up leaders around the world. They stand side by side and heart in heart with their

The Trust of Leadership

pastor as they lead a growing church, accompanying him and his wife Laura as they teach around the world and contribute to the articles in *Leadership Teaching Magazine*. They team with their pastor to mentor other church leadership teams on the power of healthy, united church leadership.

Pastor Gregg is all about raising up leaders, whether staff pastors who go on to be strong and effective church leaders or pastors who have had little or no training in leadership. For Gregg, it is all about helping men and women reach their maximum capability of bringing pleasure to God and help to God's people.

Johnson leads but he is also a great teammate. As a presbyter of the New York District of the Assemblies of God he serves as an extension of the superintendent's office to serve the credential holders and churches of the Hudson Valley. He does so with excellence and sacrifice. As a member of the leadership of the District he asks the tough questions transparently—without any personal agenda— and then solidly supports the direction of the entire team. Future and current leaders could "go to school" by living a few days with Gregg Johnson.

The expectation by others that leaders behave responsibly or honorably is the trust of leadership. Warren Bennis said, "Leadership without character is unthinkable - or should be." *The Trust of Leadership* is all about that expectation that, when present in the life of the practitioner, brings hope, success and advancement for the benefit of those being served.

I have seen Gregg Johnson lead, be led and teach on leadership. He lives out the lessons we find in this book. The principles found here will be a source of help to leaders at every level of society: government, judicial, business and church. You can trust that kind of leadership.

Duane P. Durst, D. Min.
District Superintendent, AGNYD
October 2014

INTRODUCTION

TRUST: THE CREDIBILITY OF LEADERSHIP

Authority is God's idea. He created it as an equitable means of maintaining order and stability throughout His creation. It is the right to govern, to lead, to initiate action and command others.

The ancient Romans had a tradition. When an engineer constructed an arch, as the capstone was hoisted over the structure and lowered into place, the engineer would stand under the arch demonstrating his complete confidence in his design. It was a profound expression of accountability. Rather than expecting others to become victims of his potential failure, he personally and publicly bore the consequence of whether or not he had fulfilled his duty.[1]

Even more important, and because of the accountability it provided, this tradition enabled trust. Having witnessed the architect being held accountable for his design, pedestrians would have complete trust in the arch and freely pass under or over it without concern.

In a sense, the duty of leadership is like building a Roman arch. Every decision, action, and policy a leader implements must serve the interests of the people and the organization he is called to lead. Like building an arch, the leader is developing infrastructure to cover and protect, or providing passageways to improve the society he leads. When the leader is accountable for his actions, when the integrity of his decisions are open to examination and he is made to answer for his policies, his credibility is demonstrated and people will trust both him and what he builds.

Saying that "leadership is a trust" is to say that a leader's authority exists to serve the public's interests, not the personal interests of the leader. People submit themselves to leaders, they support leaders because they trust that the leaders will have their best interests, and the interests of the organization, at heart—not the leaders' own interests. This means that a leader's actions and decisions or exercise of authority should never be intended to give that leader some personal benefits or to advance his or her own interests. When that trust of leadership is violated, we call it corruption.

Corruption is the abuse of public office or leadership position for personal gain. Corruption is when something good turns bad. It is when good leaders, who begin with noble intentions, become enticed and corrupted by sordid opportunities. It is when they cease to use their authority to serve the public good or the organizations they are charged to serve and, instead, use their position to leverage power, wealth, and privilege to themselves.

Most references to corruption usually involve grand (or political) corruption. These generally involve large sums of money, unethical government leaders, and impact an entire country. On the continent of Africa, for example, internal corruption costs nearly 150 billion dollars a year, as estimated by the African Union. Grand corruption has the ability to paralyze an entire nation's economy and decrease any future potential for growth.

To this concern, President Barack Obama, in his speech to the Ghanaian Parliament in 2009 said, "History offers a clear verdict: governments that respect the will of their own people are more prosperous, more stable, and more successful than governments that do not. No country is going to create wealth if its leaders exploit the economy to enrich themselves, or police can be bought

The Trust of Leadership

off by drug traffickers. No business wants to invest in a place where the government skims 20 percent off the top, or the head of the Port Authority is corrupt. No person wants to live in a society where the rule of law gives way to the rule of brutality and bribery. That is not democracy—that is tyranny—and now is the time for it to end. In the 21st century, capable, reliable, and transparent institutions are the key to success—strong parliaments and honest police forces; independent judges and journalists; a vibrant private sector, and civil society. Those are the things that give life to democracy, because that is what matters in peoples' lives."[2]

Corruption, however, is not limited to the likes of unscrupulous dictators. Petty corruption refers to street-level, everyday corruption that ordinary citizens experience as they interact with low- or mid-level public officials in places like hospitals, schools, police departments and other bureaucratic agencies. Although the amount of money involved may be relatively small, in many countries, it impacts the average person on a regular basis.

Almost everywhere we turn, in any profession, the trust of leadership is on the decline. Research shows that only 49% of employees trust senior management, and only 28% believe CEOs are a credible source of information. Nursing, highly rated by 82% of people, was the most trustworthy profession. Whereas, Congressmen were at the bottom of the list; only 8% of Americans believed their leaders in Washington are trustworthy. The Gallup survey also found that Americans' rating of the honesty and ethics of the clergy has fallen below 50% for the first time since 1977.[3]

This speaks to the most alarming place where corruption is seen today: church and religious institutions. This is especially predominant in Charismatic and Pentecostal circles that are often driven by flamboyant, charismatic personalities. When such individuals achieve a certain level of notoriety marked by large crowds and big offerings, their "spiritual authority" turns into celebrity fame and they use their influence, not to serve the faithful, but to enrich themselves.

The Trust of Leadership

Ephesians 4:11 teaches that the offices of apostle, prophet, evangelist, pastor, and teacher are positions of spiritual authority. Leaders in these positions, who use that authority to manipulate followers for the purpose of enriching themselves, have violated their trust and are corrupt. It could be a pastor in New York, an evangelist in the United Kingdom, or a prophet in East Africa. Any leader who enriches himself from the suffering or sacrifice of those he is supposed to be serving is a wolf in sheep's clothing. He's not there to empower, he's there to devour, and that is corrupt.

Too often, we've seen these preachers take advantage of crowds of people ranging from the poor and illiterate to the powerful and successful by promising God's blessings of wealth in return for generous offerings. Many of these spiritual leaders have little or no formal religious training, except for what they see on television (e.g., TBN), and are known to resort to tricks, gimmicks, and outright deception to demonstrate their "special anointing" and touch from God.

BBC News reported a Ghanaian pastor who arrived at Entebbe Airport in Uganda only to find police waiting for him. Local law enforcement had been informed that a Pentecostal pastor was trying to bring an electric shock device into the country. A search of his luggage revealed a magician's tool called the "Electric Touch Machine." It consisted of a battery pack, some wires and electrodes. The device amplifies static electricity on your body and enables you to deliver an electric shock to whatever (or whomever) you touch. The pastor would use it during altar calls. People would bring their offerings to the altar, then by laying hands on them, he would impart an enhanced static shock, leading them to believe they received an electrified anointing from the Holy Spirit.[4]

Another report exposed a Kenyan pastor who was arrested in London, England, for trafficking babies out of Nairobi. He claimed to have an anointed touch that enabled infertile women to become pregnant. The "miracle" involved the pastor performing an exorcism on the infertile woman which supposedly cleanses her soul, followed by his declaration that she is now pregnant. After only a couple weeks of pregnancy, the minister takes women to Nairobi to "give birth" in the slum clinics. However, DNA tests have proven that twenty-one of these "miracle babies" had no biological link to their supposed parents and further medical evidence proved the women were not pregnant before the "births." Apparently babies were taken from slum families and given to these women for whom they would pay a handsome fee.[5]

Over the past twenty years, there has been a groundswell of these corrupt preachers. One preacher claimed to have the "new car anointing." Gullible believers are told to bring a picture of the new car they desire wrapped up in a generous offering and God will provide the car. Another peddled his "new house anointing." He told his followers that God had blessed him with a supernatural ability to acquire numerous homes and properties—if they would bring an offering on a specially designated Sunday, he would give them satchels of dirt from his "divinely provided yard." In turn, they could sprinkle the dirt on their yards which would result in a miraculous provision of new properties.

Corruption can occur wherever people have power, control or influence over other people and use that power to serve themselves at the expense of another's suffering or sacrifice. Spiritual leaders, because of the trust associated with their positions, can be subject to corruption just as any politician, police officer, or CEO.

Steven Covey wrote, "The first job of any leader is to inspire trust."[6] I couldn't agree more. But while Covey goes on to correctly state that trust is born of two dimensions, character and competence, I believe there is a third: accountability. As Covey points out, character includes honesty and personal integrity which are vital to the leader; and competency refers to education, skills and capability—also essential. Accountability, however, goes further. It requires that the authority of leaders be subject to checks and balances and be answerable for their decisions and actions in order to justify them or hold them liable in cases of misconduct. Every leader who has authority must be transparent and answerable to others. This is the trust of leadership. This is standing under the arch.

Roman engineers, if not put under the arch, may have been enticed to compromise their design. Perhaps they would use cheaper materials and pocket the savings for themselves. Perhaps they would use less experienced, less qualified labor when kickbacks were provided by that company's owner. Perhaps they would neglect to add certain components knowing there would be more profit from which to personally benefit. Remove the prospect of accountability and leaders become prone to compromise and corruption.

The single greatest means of establishing trust in leadership is through accountability. When people know that leaders are answerable for their actions and their authority is kept in check, they will be willing to invest sacrificially, participate personally, and support passionately the mission of the organization.

The purpose of this book is to help leaders build a stable, enduring arch. If people are to trust our work and our leadership, there must be opportunities for us to stand under the arch and demonstrate our credibility. Materials such as transparency, reportability, fuduciarity, humility, and collegiality are the cement that makes our structure secure. Whether you're a church leader, a government official, a civic leader, or a corporate executive, these truths serve to strengthen your life's work.

The Trust of Leadership

The Trust of Leadership

CHAPTER ONE

ACCOUNTABILITY

Accountability implies answerability. It occurs when one party is obliged to report to another party regarding his or her actions and decisions in order to justify them or to suffer consequences in the case of misconduct.

Ancient history is dominated by the rule of monarchs, emperors, and Caesars. From the beginning of recorded history through the Middle Ages, most nations were controlled by some form of "royalty" regarded as absolute. Pagan nations often viewed their kings as gods in human form. Even early Christendom considered monarchs to be "king by divine right" meaning a king or queen could not be subject to any earthly authority having derived their right to rule directly from God. Elaborate coronations occurred in which popes and bishops of the church would validate a king's "divine right." These were typically nothing more than convenient accords amassing wealth to the church and limitless authority to the kings.[1]

It wasn't until A.D. 1215 when King John of England came to power that all of this would change. His inept and corrupt leadership resulted in papal excommunication and great financial losses to the nation. Frustrated by his incompetence, the land barons of Britain banded together to take action. While King John was traveling they took control of London and threatened a civil war unless he signed a document agreeing to 63 written demands. In return, the barons would pledge loyalty to the king. It was called the Magna Carta (Latin for the "Great Charter") and John had no choice but to sign it.

The Magna Carta marked the first time in history that written law challenged the absolute power of a monarch, and the first time that governments, even kings, could be held accountable for their actions. It stands through history as the symbol against oppression and the standard that those granted authority must be held accountable. So important was this truth, that it influenced the Habeas Corpus Act of England (1679), and the U.S. Constitution (1787) and Bill of Rights (1791).[2]

Accountability implies answerability. It occurs when one party is obliged to report to another party regarding his or her actions and decisions in order to justify them or to suffer punishment in the case of misconduct. In essence, it means that no one leader or group of leaders is autonomous, but they are surrounded by a system of checks and balances that places boundaries on their authority.

Accountability is the single greatest means of preserving the trust of leadership. When exercised effectively, it serves two essential functions. First, it enhances the performance of leaders and, second, it protects the organization *from* leaders. Accountability ensures that those in authority are provided with the support structures they need to perform optimally while, at the same time, keeping them in check and preventing them from abusing their power for personal gain.

TO PROTECT THE ORGANIZATION

David was a man after God's own heart. He was a gifted musician, a mighty warrior, and the most beloved man in Israel. No one in the nation could compare to the success and wealth of this man. Add to all that, he was king.

The Trust of Leadership

As king, David was sovereign. It would be a millennia before the Magna Carta, so his actions were absolute and beyond question. No one dared challenge the king's opinion or contest his will. Whatever the king wanted, the king would get. Sadly, this power, unchecked and absolute, became a tragic source of misery both in his personal life and in the nation he led.

The tragedy came from two major failures in David's life. The first was a scandalous affair with Bathsheba and the murder of her husband (2 Samuel 11). The second occurred when he numbered Israel to bring glory to himself (1 Chronicles 21). In both instances, the king was free to act without boundaries or restraint.

While it is true that Nathan rebuked David for adultery and murder, the rebuke came too late, after the heinous deeds were done. Joab warned David not to number Israel, but David was under no obligation to heed Joab. The king was free do whatever the king wanted to do. As a result, a curse was put upon David's family for his sin against Uriah and a deadly plague besieged the nation because he sought to glorify himself. It is a classic example of what happens when fallen beings are given unlimited authority.

Authority was created by God as an equitable means of maintaining order and stability throughout mankind. Authority is the right to govern, exercise leadership, initiate an action, or give commands. It flows from a position granted to an individual by a higher authority or by the consent of the governed.

Leaders have been given a sacred trust. They have a duty to govern, but such action must always be carried out with proper motive and attitude. Deuteronomy 17:14-20 explains the parameters: "The king ...shall not multiply horses for himself, ...neither shall he multiply wives for himself ...nor shall he greatly multiply silver and gold for himself ...he shall fear the LORD his God ... that his heart may not be lifted above his brethren..." In other words, the leader has been entrusted with authority, not to serve his own interests, but to serve the interests of the entity he leads and people that comprise it. Not an easy task for men and women whose hearts are "desperately wicked."

The saddest irony in the story of David is that he was chosen by God because of the goodness of his heart. The Lord directed Samuel, "Do not look at his appearance or at his physical stature... for the LORD does not see as man sees; for man looks at the outward appearance, but the LORD looks at the heart" (1 Samuel 16:7). Obviously, the Lord saw something pure, something upright, about David that qualified him as a monarch. And David was a great king, perhaps the greatest that ever lived. He ruled with wisdom, humility, righteousness, and godly fear. Unfortunately, he was still a man—a depraved fallen creature. As such, he was subject to the corruption that often occurs as a result of absolute authority.

The failures of King David demonstrates why leaders—even good leaders—need structures of accountability. Lord Acton said it like this: "Power corrupts and absolute power corrupts absolutely." Human nature is insidious. As good as a person may seem to be, if there are no restraints or restrictions, if a person is free to act without any accountability or answerability, that person will be corrupted by his own depraved desire and driven to satisfy his own carnal interests. Jeremiah 17:9 says, "The heart is deceitful above all things, And desperately wicked." It is a sad fact of human nature: power without accountability corrupts.

This is what Edmund Burke meant when he wrote, "Those who have been once intoxicated with power, and have derived any kind of emolument from it, never can willingly abandon it." In other words, authority is like an inebriant that intoxicates a leader with an illicit sense of power; and having tasted that power, he or she becomes addicted to it and abuses it. Many leaders, who began with pure hearts and noble intentions, become inebriated by their command over people and intoxicated by a perverted sense of power. Their egos inflate with self-importance, they become blind with ambition and they start to think, "Because I am the leader, because I am the one with the title, the one with the authority, I am more important than those who are under me. They exist to serve me." To such leaders, authority is no longer a sacred trust facilitating care and protection to those in need. Instead, it becomes a means to exploit others for the leader's own ambitions. We see it in David. As king, he had a solemn responsibility to serve and protect the rights of his citizens. As king, he should have served Bathsheba, defended Uriah, and put Israel before himself. Instead, he used his authority to serve his own interests at the expense of Bathsheba and Uriah, and seventy-thousand who died in a plague of judgment. David became corrupt.

But was it authority that corrupted David? Or, was it the lack of accountability that corrupted him? Obviously, the latter. Had David known that his authority was in check, had he known he was obliged to answer for his actions, had he known he would have to explain himself to others and justify his actions or suffer consequences for misconduct, it is very likely we would be telling a very different story about David today. David would have been protected from himself.

TO ENHANCE PERFORMANCE

Rehoboam had some very big shoes to fill. His father, King Solomon, was the wisest, wealthiest, and most powerful man in the world. Upon his death, Rehoboam became king and immediately his wisdom was tested.

Scripture tells us the whole assembly of Israel gathered to him and said, "Your father made our yoke heavy; now therefore, lighten the burdensome service of your father, and his heavy yoke which he put on us, and we will serve you" (1 Kings 12:4). Fortunately, Rehoboam had Solomon's wise counselors at his disposal. All he needed was to consult them and follow their guidance. Surely, they had gleaned insight from Solomon and understood Israel well enough to know what they needed. Unfortunately, Rehoboam rejected their advice and did the exact opposite.

The young king, after consulting his young inexperienced friends, proclaimed to Israel: "My father made your yoke heavy, but I will add to your yoke; my father chastised you with whips, but I will chastise you with scourges!" (1 Kings 12:14). Obviously, this news was not received well by the populace. Ten of the tribes broke away from Rehoboam's rule and formed the new, northern confederacy of Israel. Rehoboam was left with two tribes to rule and remained in Jerusalem; his southern confederacy would be called the Nation of Judah.

The failure of King Rehoboam demonstrates what can happen when a leader operates without accountability. He loses the benefit of wise counsel. Accountability not only protects the leader from corruption, it surrounds him with people who can speak into his life giving him guidance, inspiration, and counsel to improve his performance as a leader.

Accountability is not an obstacle on your path to success, it is the guardrail that gets you there safely. Rehoboam thought the elderly counsel would slow him down, but it was actually meant to preserve him. This is true, not only of executive leaders, but of every person in any organization. Accountability should be seen as a part of your life structure giving you stability and support; not a vehicle to tear down and destroy. We all need people around us to whom we must answer for our actions and from whom we receive criticism. This will be explained more in Chapter Six: Collegiality.

DEFINING ACCOUNTABILITY

There is often a lot of excitement around the topic of accountability. In fact, it is quite in vogue. Having an accountability partner is very stylish. In fact, if you're a leader and don't make yourself accountable to some group of confidants, you're not very fashionable. Unfortunately, these notions of accountability, although helpful to some, do not rise to the level of maintaining the trust of leadership.

True accountability is not a cozy relationship that the leader turns on and off at his own whim. It's not merely a group of friends who gather for prayer and Bible study over coffee and ask four or five personal questions. True accountability is systemic. It is built into the structure of the organization. It is part of the organizational DNA and demands the participation and submission of the leader on a regular, formal basis. True accountability cannot be avoided, put off, delayed, or shut down. In trustworthy, credible, healthy organizations, it is a predominate feature of the culture.

By the same token, accountability is not some legalistic tribunal where victims are humiliated and devalued. It is not meant to provide a forum where authorities are "put-in-their-place" by power-hungry, small-minded, authority-grabbing bullies who think they have some perverted right to lord themselves over their leaders. Such individuals undermine the integrity of the organization because they give accountability a bad name. They are part of the problem. Leaders welcome accountability when administered by trusted individuals whom they know have the best interests of both the leader and the organization in mind. But they will be reluctant to freely participate in a system that caters to a mob of co-dependent bullies seeking a chance to flex their fragile egos.

So what is accountability and how is it expressed in a healthy organization? The following are four basic elements of accountability as expressed in trustworthy entities.

ACCOUNTABILITY REQUIRES ANSWERABILITY

Every trustworthy leader shares one common quality: answerability. As well, every trustworthy organization has leaders who are answerable. In other words, leaders are obligated to report to others regarding their actions and decisions. It means that the leader is required to explain himself in order to justify his actions or to suffer consequences in the case of misconduct. Organizations that are trustworthy have leaders who are surrounded by others having the right and responsibility to question them.

By contrast, those in leadership positions are described as unaccountable when they are under no requirement to explain themselves or take responsibility for their actions. What they need to realize is that if King John of England had to sign the Magna Carta and answer for his decisions, so does the local pastor, the office manager, the senator, and the CEO. No one leader is beyond answerability.

Even David, although king, made himself answerable for his actions. The prophet Nathan cried out, "You are the man. You despised the commandment of the Lord and did evil in His sight!" (2 Samuel 12:7-9). In an act of exemplary humility, David submitted to the charge and accepted the blame. He became answerable.

Answerability is being transparent and reporting fully. It is providing all information needed to bring others into a full understanding of the issues at hand. It is full disclosure. Rather than withholding information and allowing people to arrive at a false conclusion, those who are answerable offer what may have remained hidden to ensure that their integrity and honesty remains intact.

Answerability is more than merely passively hearing someone else's criticism on a matter—it is taking full responsibility and accepting the burden for whatever the outcome. It is morally obligating one's self to what could have been done, what should have been done, and accepting the blame for inaction or wrong action.

Answerable people do not shift the blame to others. They do not make excuses or become defensive. They admit their culpability, learn from their mistakes, and pledge to do better. This is the essence of accountability. It is taking ownership of the expectations and demands assigned, assumed, or imposed to us and personally owning the consequences of whether or not we have fulfilled those demands.

In order for answerability to exist, there must be those around the leader who have been vested with the right and responsibility to call him to account. It requires a balance of power.

ACCOUNTABILITY REQUIRES A BALANCE OF POWER

The highest safeguard against the corruption of leadership is a system of checks and balances that keeps leadership fair and just. In 1 Peter 5:5, the apostle commanded those in authority to "be submissive to one another, and be clothed with humility, for 'God resists the proud, but gives grace to the humble.'" God's model for authority intends that leaders be mutually submissive to one another rather than lord their position in autonomous sovereignty.

The concept of "Checks and Balances" originated in ancient Greece and has been incorporated into modern democracies to ensure a balance of power in government. For example, when America's founding fathers won independence from England's oppressive monarchy, they wanted a system to ensure that no one person could become all-powerful in "ruling" the country. "Checks and Balances" is a structure of multiple branches of government (executive, legislative, and judicial) which limit each other's power and require mutual accountability. In other words, every leader is kept in check by corresponding leaders who balance one another's power.

Wherever countries have maintained governments with minimal corruption, there have been efficient means of checks and balances. On the contrary, whenever such accountability and limitation of power is absent, ruling parties inevitably abuse and become authoritarian. The result is usually a corrupt government with a dictator who ravages the economy.

This is not merely a dynamic of secular government; it is an ever present reality of human nature, even in church leadership. Ronald Enroth, in his book, *Churches That Abuse*, wrote, "Spiritual abuse can take place in the context of doctrinally sound, Bible-preaching, fundamentalist, conservative Christianity. All that is needed for abuse is a pastor accountable to no one and therefore beyond confrontation."[3]

The biblical model for church leadership addresses this. Nowhere does scripture teach that any one leader is absolute in his authority. In fact, the model Paul laid out was one of "plurality in leadership." He told Timothy to ordain elders in every city which would provide a balance of power, or checks and balances. The pastor is to be "first among equals." In modern terms we find this principle expressed in the use of various leadership positions (trustees, council members, directors, deacons, etc.) who serve alongside the pastor. While one may argue the accuracy of these modern titles to the biblical function of an elder or overseer, the principle of checks and balances applies. Whatever the term, the need for a balance of power is implied and must therefore be provided. To achieve this effectively, it must be defined in the entity's organizational structure.

ACCOUNTABILITY REQUIRES STRUCTURAL INTEGRITY

When a dictator comes to power, the first thing he does is dismantle structures of accountability.

In 1971, Idi Amin seized control of the Ugandan government. Within days, the self-proclaimed "President for Life" massacred anyone he perceived as a threat to his power. Entire brigades of soldiers were slaughtered as were religious leaders, journalists, senior bureaucrats, judges, intellectuals, and anyone who challenged his actions or questioned his decisions. So widespread were the killings that the amount of bodies floating down the Nile River threatened to clog the nation's hydro-electric dam. For eight years, Amin's murderous oppression went unchecked amassing a death toll over 500,000.

In 1993, General Sani Abacha came to power in Nigeria. Upon doing so, he shut down all democratic structures, dissolved the free press, and jailed voices of dissent under charge of treason. Opposing political parties were outlawed and elected government officials were replaced by subservient military commanders. To solidify his authority, Abacha surrounded himself with 3,000

The Trust of Leadership

armed thugs loyal to his every command. It was in this vacuum of accountability that the general allowed the exploitation of Nigerian land by multinational oil companies for which he was generously rewarded while murdering or imprisoning activists who challenged him. During Abacha's Regime, a total of £3 billion was siphoned out of the country's coffers earning Abacha the ignominious listing as the world's fourth most corrupt leader of his time.

Leaders, and the organizations they serve, derive their credibility from the integrity of the structures that support them. Aside from the atrocities committed by Idi Amin and Sani Abacha, these men had no credibility because there were no structures of integrity around them. The judiciary was dismantled, the free press was shut down, dissenting voices were silenced, and democratic systems were dissolved. Any objective person looking in from the outside would immediately dismiss these men as untrustworthy.

It is not enough for leaders to agree with the notions of accountability. There must be formalized structures in the organization, beyond their own control, that mandate accountability on a regular consistent basis. We repel accountability by nature. If left to ourselves, we'll do what we want to do. It's the structures, standing on their own, that perpetuate the trust of the organization beyond the leader's initiative.

The first structure is the Constitution and Bylaws. The Constitution identifies the fundamental principles which govern an organization's operation. The bylaws establish the rules by which the group is to function. Before an entity can be considered credible and trustworthy, it must lay down this basic structure and methods of operation in writing.

One provision of the bylaws is to define roles and set limits upon positions of authority. They explain certain elements such as positions of authority, limits of authority, checks and balances, reporting, and processes for significant decisions. It is from this standard that all other means of accountability derive their power.

Another structure of authority is the Board of Directors.

Sometimes called trustees, these individuals make up the governing body and hold the fiduciary trust of the organization. Usually elected by the constituency, they ensure that the interests of the constituency are protected. The directors provide guidance regarding operational issues, mitigate legal issues, review financial statements, and establish policy. The board is the primary agent of accountability within the organization as they provide checks and balances for the chairman or CEO.

A third vehicle of organizational integrity is transparency or open reporting. When something is "transparent" you can see into it clearly and examine it closely. Nothing is hidden or concealed. In organizational terms, transparency is allowing the open examination of practices and policies to prevent abuses. It's when budgets and financial statements can be reviewed and decisions are open to discussion, or even criticism. Such a culture of openness prevents the opportunity for authorities to abuse the system for their own interests or set damaging policies.

ACCOUNTABILITY REQUIRES FAIRNESS AND IMPARTIALITY

Systems of accountability often fall apart when the leader surrounds himself or herself with people who are biased toward the leader. In other words, if the structures of answerability surrounding a leader are to be credible, they must be administered by people who do not personally benefit by maintaining the power of the leader. For accountability to work, it must be impartial.

Nepotism comes from the 14th century Roman word "nepotismo." It referred to a practice in the Catholic Church during the Middle Ages when popes and bishops gave their "nephews" positions of preference in church hierarchy. Many of these so-called nephews were actually illegitimate sons of popes who violated their vows of chastity and made such appointments as a means to continue their papal "dynasty." The practice became so widespread that the "Cardinal Nephew System" was a fully accepted part of the papal life until reformed in the 17th century. It should be noted that these "nephew cardinals" were known to be immature and quite incompetent. They were notorious for amassing wealth and leveraging their positions to advance personal interests.

Simply put, nepotism is the favoring of relatives. It occurs when those in authority prefer relatives in the bestowal of offices on the grounds of relationship rather than merit. Examples can be found in church, government, and business when one hires, appoints, or promotes family members solely because they are family members, without considering the qualifications of other candidates for those positions.

Every nation has a history of nepotism. America's 19th president, Rutherford B. Hayes, declared, "No person connected with me by blood or marriage will be appointed to office." His firm stand against nepotism was one way he hoped to clean up Washington after the corruption-filled administration of his predecessor, Ulysses S. Grant.

But nepotism has never been easy to banish from American—or, for that matter, any nation's—politics. Even the United States' founding fathers, despite their opposition to hereditary privileges, found ways to advance their relatives' careers in public office. A more recent example was President John F. Kennedy who appointed his own brother Robert as attorney general in 1961. It wasn't until 1967 that the U.S. Congress passed an anti-nepotism statute that prohibited government officials from employing, promoting or appointing any relative to a position in the agency where the public official serves.

Nepotism undermines the credibility of an organization. It reinforces the notion that an organization or government exists to serve the interests of those in power. Rather than appointing those who are best qualified to build and benefit the system, the system is manipulated to build dynasties of those who are in power.

While conducting conferences in Nigeria, I was struck by the

The Trust of Leadership

blatant practice of nepotism in one church's leadership structure. It was a huge facility with a seating capacity of 8,000. However, the leadership team was limited to a tiny collection of family members. The pastor was the chairman of the board, his wife was a trustee, his brother was the treasurer, his sister was the secretary, and other director positions were held by additional relatives. The pastor rationalized this structure by explaining that he couldn't trust anyone but family members to be loyal to him and maintain a healthy financial and management structure.

Seriously? In a church of 8,000 people he can find no one, aside from family members, to be qualified to fill these positions? It sounds more like this pastor has become a Pentecostal dictator who built a dynastic power block over the church free from accountability and beyond confrontation.

From my perspective as a prospective donor or supporter of his ministry, I have no confidence in the integrity of this organization. Using family members creates a conflict of interest. Because their appointments and employment hinges on their relationship to the pastor, how can they be trusted to ever question, challenge or criticize his decisions as such actions may destabilize his power and undermine their job security. They have a personal interest in strengthening his authority and are more likely to act only in ways that support and embolden his power. Due to the lack of integrity in this organization, Global Leadership Training no longer associates with them.

FINAL THOUGHT

Accountability occurs when one is obligated to answer for his actions, either to justify them or face penalties for misconduct. It means no one leader or group of leaders is sovereign, but their authority is held in check.

The single greatest means of establishing trust in leadership is through accountability. When people know that leaders are answerable for their actions and their authority is kept in check, they will be willing to invest sacrificially, participate personally, and support passionately the mission of the organization.

CHAPTER TWO

TRANSPARENCY

A lack of transparency is a sign of unhealth and manipulation. When leaders avoid transparency, it's usually because they are trying to get away with something that would be considered immoral or unethical by most people.

Before it filed for bankruptcy in 2000, the Enron Corporation employed over 20,000 people and reported revenues of over $100 billion. So great was its "success" that Enron was named "America's Most Innovative Company" by *Fortune* magazine for six consecutive years. Unfortunately, what was perceived as lucrative success was actually a deliberate attempt to deceive investors from the facts of its dire financial health.

The genius behind Enron's deception was in the creative accounting of its CEO, Kenneth Lay. Rather than providing full disclosure of assets and liabilities to investors, he set up numerous subsidiaries that allowed Enron to hide its debts and grow its stock price. Essentially, whatever risks, liabilities, and losses existed were absent from Enron's financial statements. Any assets that were listed were actually fraudulent or, at best, severely inflated.

By the time the U.S. Securities and Exchange Commission completed its investigation, Enron had over $38 billion in hidden debt resulting in a $74 billion loss to its shareholders and billions lost in employee pension benefits. Enron's collapse, and the ensuing financial havoc, led to new regulations mandating the accuracy of financial reporting and escalating the consequences for destroying, altering or fabricating financial records of publically-held companies.

When something is "transparent" you can see into it clearly and examine it closely. Nothing is hidden or concealed. In organizational terms, transparency is allowing the open examination of practices and policies to prevent abuses. It's when budgets and financial statements can be reviewed and decisions are open to discussion, or even criticism. Such a culture of openness prevents the opportunity for authorities to abuse the system for their own interests or set damaging policies.

There is no more fundamental expression of an organization's integrity than transparency. When leaders allow open access to financial records and scrutiny of internal processes, it demonstrates their commitment to uprightness. Transparency reveals their willingness to be held accountable and keep their authority in check, ensuring they use their position to serve the organization—not themselves. Without transparency and the accountability it provides, authority tends to twist leaders into self-serving dictators abusing power for their own gain. It's a fact of history. Transparency is the first causality of a dictatorship. Wherever a dictator existed—or exists—transparency must be eliminated so the leader can operate without checks and balances on his authority.

Unfortunately, dictators can rise to power in any context of authority, not just political. Accordingly, transparency must be present wherever men or women are given the power to command others and expend resources. The following are some prime examples.

Governmental Transparency is the means of holding public officials accountable and reducing opportunities for corruption. It occurs when a government's meetings are open to the public and the press. More importantly, transparency in government is when budgets and spending may be reviewed by anyone, and its laws and decisions are open to discussion and criticism.

Transparency is especially important concerning government procurement of goods and services. From building highways to furnishing hospitals to selling mineral rights, these transactions often exceed 30 percent of some governments' gross domestic product. This often brings easy opportunities for corruption. In fact, Transparency International reports that, on average, as much as 25 percent of procurement funds disappear into the private coffers of corrupt government officials.[1]

It's only when procurement of government contracts is transparent, and the process can be effectively monitored by the public, that corruption is discouraged and a level playing field for bidders is established in procurement process.

Military Transparency can be difficult, especially when certain programs are classified as secret to preserve national security. Even in such cases, vehicles of transparency must be in place to eliminate corruption and abuse of military power. Many countries rely on governmental oversight committees that monitor military missions while preserving confidentiality. Such a system offers a way to provide transparency without exposing vital secrets.

Corporate Transparency is facilitating easy public access to corporate information in order to fully inform individuals or organizations that seek to participate in, or invest in, that corporation. It is quite possible that a corporation could act immorally by focusing solely on the financial "bottom line." Such an approach disregards ethical responsibilities (e.g., environmental or humanitarian) as well as overlooking the company's stakeholders. Immoral corporations manipulate by withholding information and causing people to act in a way they would not typically act if they had all the information. Corporations that exhibit transparency desire to have a good, ethical reputation. They provide very clear financial statements, frank descriptions of policies, and candid disclosures of assets, risks, and liabilities.

Studies suggest that corporate transparency pays. According to Robert Eccles, author of *The Value Reporting Revolution*, the market gives a higher value to firms that are upfront with investors and analysts.[2] Eccles shows that companies with fuller disclosure win more trust from investors. Relevant and reliable information means less risk to investors and thus a lower cost of capital, which naturally translates into higher valuations. The bottom line is people value honesty and integrity, and the best way for a corporation to demonstrate its integrity is by providing full transparency.

Non-governmental Organizations (NGOs) and Non-Profits have a particular interest in providing transparency due to their responsibilities towards both the cause they serve and the donors (often including corporations and governments) who fund the cause. Unfortunately, many NGOs are severely lacking in transparency, especially in the United States.

From 2007 to 2010, the U.S. Senate Finance Committee investigated six prominent televangelist ministries for possible financial misconduct.[3] The committee's report released by Iowa Senator Chuck Grassley raised questions about the personal use of church-owned airplanes, luxury homes, and credit cards by pastors and their families. It also expressed concerns about the lack of oversight of finances by boards often packed with the televangelists' relatives and friends.[4] The committee asked the ministries to provide financial information to determine whether or not ministry funds were used inappropriately by ministry leaders. Two of the ministries allowed limited review while the other four refused to cooperate.

While some have raised concerns that the finance committee's investigation was an abuse of power, the larger issue is a lack of transparency. If the ministries had a culture of openness and transparency, Senator Grassley would have never had to conduct an investigation—the information would have been readily available. Furthermore, had they been operating with transparency, the alleged abuses, such as nepotism and misappropriation of funds, would probably not even have occurred. It is to this point that the Apostle Paul wrote in 2 Corinthians 8:21 that we should provide all things honorable, not only in the sight of the Lord, but also in the sight of men.

What about Media Transparency? Scandals such as Enron, political abuses, and televangelists' lavish lifestyles often put the issue of transparency in the forefront of the news. But this begs several questions, "How transparent are the media? Is there a bias among certain news agencies? Are there conflicts of interest among reporters and, if so, do the media outlets disclose them?"

According to a study on "Openness and Accountability" done by the International Center for Media and Public Agenda, most news outlets are unwilling to let the public see how their editorial process works. Even worse, many internationally-renowned media outlets received a "poor" rating when it came to their own transparency.[5] The study used five categories to evaluate the news outlets: 1. Corrections—Willingness to openly correct mistakes; 2. Ownership—Openness about corporate ownership; 3. Staff Policies—Openness about conflicts of interest; 4. Reporting Policies—Openness about editorial guidelines; and 5. Interactivity—Openness to reader comments and criticism. Just to name a few, *Time* magazine rated a "0.6," FoxNews rated a "1.2," and CNN rated a "1" which all are considered "poor" ratings. MSNBC and the *Wall Street Journal* both rated a "2" which is considered "good." Whereas *The Guardian* earned a "3.8" and the *New York Times* rated a "3.4" which are both ratings of "excellent."

Transparency is a function of accountability. It implies that the organization, together with its leader and his team, are subject to inspection. Even more, it demonstrates that the system in place allows the leader's practices, policies, and decisions to be open to scrutiny, criticism, even disagreement. Essentially, it means that an organization—and its leaders—are healthy, ethical, and trustworthy.

By contrast, the lack of transparency is a sign of unhealth and manipulation. When leaders avoid transparency, it's usually because they are trying to get away with something that would be considered immoral or unethical by most people. The absence of transparency means leaders are hiding the fact that they are misusing their authority for personal benefit and not for the public's good or the good of the organization they are called to lead. Plainly stated, the lack of transparency is an indication of corruption. It is a sure sign that those in authority are keeping things in the dark because exposure would result in criticism or even expulsion.

So how can an organization maintain its credibility as an ethical and trustworthy entity? How can leaders maintain their own integrity and avoid the very appearance of scandal? The next chapter provides practical guidelines for leaders who are serious about this issue.

The Trust of Leadership

The Trust of Leadership

CHAPTER THREE

REPORTABILITY

Reportability is the quality of being reportable. It is a willingness to provide sufficient information that brings others into an accurate understanding of the matters at hand.

Yoido Full Gospel Church, located in Seoul Korea, is known as the world's largest megachurch with a membership of nearly 1 million souls. Led by Pastor David Yong-gi Cho, it has become the standard in mobilizing a congregation to prayer, developing a titanic network of bible study groups, and impacting a nation for the gospel. Unfortunately, it has also joined the nefarious list of churches embroiled in financial scandal.[1]

In 2012, an investigative team of twelve Yoido Full Gospel Elders announced that founder and Emeritus Pastor David Yong-gi Cho was responsible for a failed investment of church funds incurring $29.1 million in losses. The fact-finding body of twelve elders revealed in a report to a body of 1,319 fellow elders that Cho was pressured by his eldest son, Hee-jun, to approve the purchase of stocks in a company he owned along with numerous other investment schemes. Hee-jun Cho is believed to have orchestrated the plan to recover massive losses he racked up from previous, unsuccessful stock investments. Obviously, and tragically, the money used to finance this scandal came from the donations of church members.[2]

Perhaps the most telling part of the allegations raised by the elders is the bizarre $18 million severance payment Pastor Cho allegedly received when he resigned in 2008. They claimed to have no knowledge of this payment as it was never reported to them. As well, they claimed to have no information regarding the whereabouts of over $11 million paid to the pastor between 2004 and 2008 for "special missionary expenses."[3]

As a result of the inquiry, David Yong-gi Cho was found guilty by a South Korean court for committing breach of trust and corruption amounting to $12 million. He received a suspended sentence of three years in prison with a five-year probation and was ordered to pay a penalty of $4.7 million by Seoul Central District Court. Cho's son, Hee-jun, was sentenced to three years in prison.[4]

Quoted in the South Korean newspaper, *The Korea Herald*, Kim Seong-jun, head of the committee, said "The Cho family has violated a principle rule of the church: subjecting all investment deals to approval by the internal council."[5] Reportability is the quality of being reportable. It is a willingness to provide sufficient information that brings others into an accurate understanding of the matters at hand. Reportability is the presence of financial statements revealing income and outflow. Reportability is minutes of meetings conducted by leaders who make policy and the disclosures of conflicts of interest. It is the auditing of financial records and the willingness of leaders to formally make themselves accountable for their actions.

Trust in an organization cannot be established without reportability. It helps prevent the abuse of authority while exposing those leaders who do abuse. This flows from biblical principles. John 3:19-21 reminds us, "…this is the condemnation, that the light has come into the world, and men loved darkness rather than light, because their deeds were evil. For everyone practicing evil hates the light and does not come to the light, lest his deeds should be exposed. But he who does the truth comes to the light, that his deeds may be clearly seen..."

Sadly, the natural condition of fallen man is to conceal his activities so he can act selfishly. But those who desire to rise above their corrupt human nature will "come to the light." That is, they will welcome systems of reportability that shine the light on their activity which encourage their own honesty and promote a culture of integrity. When leaders know there will be financial statements, audits, and physical inspection of their activity, there is a strong deterrent for corruption.

Unfortunately, many leaders today are threatened by reportability and the transparency it creates. Insecure leaders take offense and say, "Don't you trust me?" But they fail to understand several important principles of reportability. First, leaders who "report" demonstrate their own credibility. The more one resists transparency, the more others become convinced that the leader must be examined and closely scrutinized. By contrast, the more a leader is willing to report, the more others become convinced of his integrity and trust him to do the right thing without having to report it.

Second, reportability is not meant to protect the money from the leader—it is meant to protect the leader from the money. In other words, reportability provides a defense against accusations of impropriety. Leaders should be able to easily produce documentation that absolves them of any financial mischief because of the detailed records they keep. Even the Apostle Paul, in 1 Thessalonians 2:10, cited this kind of openness as a basis for his own credibility when he wrote, "You are witnesses, and God also, how devoutly and justly and blamelessly we behaved ourselves among you who believe."

Third, as leaders create a culture of transparency through their reportability, the more likely people will be to invest in their organization. The number one reason why the World Bank and the

International Monetary Fund withhold support from nations is their lack of transparency in reporting. When presidents become dictators who resist accountability and governments hide their corruption from reportability, intelligent investors will run. By contrast, those who encourage transparency will be regarded as healthy and credible. People will trust that organization and become willing to participate in it and invest in it personally.

Fourth, some leaders feel they are too small to develop structures of reportability. They say, "I only receive a few dollars each week, or a small amount of schillings, why should I bother with such elaborate systems of accountability?" Jesus said if you are faithful in little, you will become ruler over much (Matthew 25:23). In other words, if you can't be faithful with the few dollars you have, why should you be trusted with many dollars? The time to establish structures of reportability is not after you've acquired riches, it's now, in the place of small beginnings. Demonstrate your integrity now, begin now with systems of transparency in the place of "smallness" and show your faithfulness. By doing so, you will establish a culture of integrity that can support the enlargement that is certain to come.

Reportability is the framework of transparency in leadership. It is the tangible structure that demonstrates our integrity and enables the trust of others. The following are several specific components of reportability.

THE BUDGET

The budget is a plan for spending that is balanced by anticipated revenue. It is a proactive, financial strategy that addresses operational expenses, salaries, and ministry objectives while ending the fiscal year with a net income rather than a deficit. Without a budget, it is impossible to provide disciplined controls that ensure the integrity of the leadership while maintaining fiscal health for the organization.

First a credible budget must be developed. Every sound budg-

The Trust of Leadership

et begins with a responsible projection of income. This includes receipts from tithes, offerings, and special projects such as missions, building funds, and capital improvement campaigns. Consideration may also be given to existing reserves that can be allocated for other anticipated expenses. It should be noted that receipts designated for specific purposes must be used for those purposes. Not doing so seriously undermines the credibility of the ministry and can be considered a "misappropriation of funds."

A responsible budget will also make realistic projections regarding anticipated expenses. These projections should be based upon actual expenses of the previous year together with the growing needs of the organization. Such needs include: overhead (rent, mortgage, utilities, and maintenance); salaries (determined by an executive committee); administrative costs (including office expenses); promotion and advertising; and additional subsidies requested by supporting departments. Not insignificant to these considerations are ministry objectives germane to the vision of the organization (special events, training opportunities, projects, etc.).

Once a budget is developed, it must be approved. The budget should not be created solely by the pastor or leader. Rather, it should be developed in collaboration with a finance committee appointed by the leadership board. After the committee has developed a budget based upon the above points, it should submit its first draft to the leadership board for approval. This board should have the opportunity to question the finance committee or require changes. In a church setting, after approval by the board, the budget is usually received by the congregation for implementation. This is where reportability is demonstrated. Having the congregation's affirmation, it becomes the "financial road map" for the coming year. Even more important, it provides a blanket of protection for all in leadership, especially the leaders when it is maintained.

Finally, no budget is credible unless it is enforced. The board of directors or church treasurer is usually responsible for enforcing the budget and presenting budgetary revisions as needed. This means that each line item in the budget must be inspected on a regular basis to ensure that the manager of that line item is maintaining spending limits. If limits are compromised, consideration must be given toward revising the line item, allowing a deficit or correcting unhealthy spending habits.

FINANCIAL REPORTS

Every organization should prepare thorough and accurate financial statements. These are the primary vehicles of reporting and key components of transparency in any organization. Monthly, quarterly, and even annual, financial reports should be available for review by all invested parties.

Having a financial report, however, is not enough. The report itself must have specific elements. The Governmental Accounting Standards Board, an agency that exists to improve standards of state and local governmental accounting and financial reporting, outlines seven basic elements of financial statements for state and local governments which can be applied to other organizations.[6]

The fundamental components outlined are as follows: 1. Assets are resources with present service capacity that the organization presently controls; 2. Liabilities are present obligations to sacrifice resources that the organization has little or no discretion to avoid; 3. A deferred outflow of resources is a consumption of net assets by the organization that is applicable to a future reporting period; 4. A deferred inflow of resources is an acquisition of net assets by the organization that is applicable to a future reporting period; 5. Net position is the residual of all other elements presented in a statement of financial position; 6. An outflow of resources is a consumption of net assets by the organization that is applicable to the reporting period; 7. An inflow of resources is an acquisition of net assets by the organization that is applicable to the reporting period.

FINANCIAL AUDITS, REVIEWS AND COMPILATIONS

In addition to consistent and comprehensive financial statements, organizations should conduct regular inspections of their financial activity by an outside, independent agent. Such a practice helps ensure, and is evidence of, genuine financial accountability, especially to an organization's constituencies. These inspections can come in three forms depending on the condition of the organization.

A "Compilation" is the most rudimentary level of inspection to financial statements. In a compilation, the independent agent conducts a limited inspection of financial reports to determine if there are any obvious departures from generally accepted accounting principles. Upon completion, a report is issued that states a compilation was performed, but no assurance is given that the statements comply with generally accepted accounting principles. This is called an expression of "no assurance." Compilations are typically prepared for privately-held entities that do not need a higher level of assurance.

A "Review" is more thorough than a compilation. In addition to inspecting financial statements, the independent agent conducts certain analytical procedures to ascertain if the organization is in conformity with generally accepted accounting procedures. This often requires the agent to review certain processes and procedures within the organization associated with its cash flow. Because it is less comprehensive than an audit, the review process will only provide an expression of "limited assurance" that there is compliance with general accounting practices. A review is often prepared for organizations seeking bank loans, investors, or are somehow required to demonstrate their financial integrity.

The "Audit" is the highest level of inspection. It includes all of the work covered in a compilation and review but also conducts procedures of verification and substantiation. This includes verifying accounts, reviewing invoices and receipts, inspecting inventories, securities, board minutes, and contracts, etc. Furthermore, an audit will evaluate the organization's systems of internal control or lack thereof. When the audit is completed, a report is issued to verify an audit was performed in accordance with generally accepted auditing procedures and expresses an opinion regarding the credibility of the entity's financial condition and internal operations. This is known as an expression of "positive assurance."

TRUSTEE MEETING MINUTES

It has already been stated that trouble in an organization can usually be traced back to a failure in governance. This is especially true as it relates to directors and trustees. The board of directors is the first deterrent against the abuse of authority within an organization by mandating and establishing a culture of transparency. There are two factors that are essential for the board to do this effectively.

First, there must be regular meetings of the Board of Directors. Whether they occur monthly or quarterly, there must be ample time for board members to meet together, review financial statements, establish policy, and review the health of the organization. Boards who fail to meet and review such items are derelict of duty. They have failed in matters of due diligence.

Second, the board must keep minutes of their meetings and make them available for public review.

The "minutes" are the written record of the board's deliberations and decisions while in session. According to the Evangelical Council for Financial Accountability (ECFA), minutes should contain the following components: a list of board members present as well as those absent; the meeting's location, start time, ending time; a record of actions taken by the board with enough discussion to substantiate the actions taken; the abstention of interested parties when necessary.[7] Unless there are exceptional matters that require executive session, board minutes should be transparent.

That is, they should be available to any member of the organization who wishes to review them.

Boards who fail to provide minutes are subject to suspicion on two levels. First, they are suspect of incompetence. Some boards may feel that keeping minutes is an unnecessary task and a waste of time. On the contrary, it is an expression of organizational excellence as well as the maturity and responsibility of its leaders. Personally, I have no regard for any organization that is not managed by a capable and diligent board of directors as demonstrated by accurate record keeping and reportability.

Second, they are suspect of corruption. Boards who do not provide details of their decisions and policies make themselves vulnerable to accusation. Anyone can accuse them of setting policy and making decisions that benefit themselves or those close to them. Having detailed minutes, however, provides a written record that can prove why decisions were made and how policies were established.

A SPECIAL CONCERN FOR CHURCH LEADERS

One area where reportability is of specific concern is the church. As exemplified at the beginning of this chapter, there are far too many reports of "God's people" misappropriating or embezzling funds. If there is any area where financial integrity and reportability should be demonstrated, it should be in the church.

For example, in Oklahoma, a Pentecostal pastor was charged with embezzling thousands from the small congregation he led for eighteen months. He stands accused of writing up to $75,000 in checks from the account of his forty-member church. Elsewhere, a church member filed a lawsuit against his church to expose what happened to the $24,000 he donated to the choir. He is concerned that the money was diverted to a business interest of the pastor. In Ohio, members of a large Baptist church sued the family of their late pastor for $1 million and accused him of "diverting church money" for his private use. In a neighboring city, another pastor was sentenced to seven years in prison for stealing at least $10,000 from the Sunday collections. And, in North Carolina, two preachers were recently sentenced to prison over an $8.5 million embezzlement scheme. Charges include twenty-six counts of fraud, money laundering, and conspiracy to obstruct justice.

While the overwhelming majority of church leaders manage finances with integrity, there will always be a handful that do not. The Apostle Paul spoke of those who "peddle" the Word of God for profit (2 Corinthians 2:17). Even Jesus' financial secretary was a "thief...and used to take what was put in the money bag" for his own use (John 12:6). Most likely, these leaders did not enter ministry with ill motives. They probably began with pure hearts that desired to glorify God. However, their character eroded as questionable accounting policies brought unethical compromises and moral indiscretions. Eventually, these "indiscretions" became more than just bad decisions—they became blatantly immoral. As time grew their ministries, so did their income and pragmatic shrewdness until, with their integrity gone, they were nothing more than criminals with clerical titles. They are Men of God who have betrayed their sacred trust and sold out to carnal impulse.

RECEIVING AN OFFERING OR EXTORTION THROUGH INIMIDATION?

We hear it all the time: "Sow your money into this ministry today," the flamboyant preacher proclaims, "and you will reap a harvest of blessing. Miss this opportunity and you may never receive the miracle you need." When the baskets were passed, people gave liberally, convinced that their giving will bring God's blessing. Even worse, to not give would result in lack.

The legal world defines extortion as obtaining money or goods from another through intimidation, manipulation or threats. While no one is threatening bodily harm or holding a gun to anyone's head—the words spoken by the "Man of God" have the same effect. People are intimidated through fear, manipulated by emotion, and threatened by "the Word of God" to give their money right now or suffer ambiguous consequences. It may not be considered extortion in a court of law—but it is in the spirit. What looks like a normal church offering is a shameful attempt to extort money from the people of God.

This is not to say that church leaders should never receive offerings. On the contrary, the principles of God's Word regarding stewardship and tithing must be taught and people should be encouraged to give. Paul instructed the Corinthian church to receive offerings on every first day of the week (1 Corinthians 16:2). Public offerings are a powerful expression of worship and a scriptural way to give thanks for God's bounty. With regard to receiving offerings, the issue for leaders is one of motive and technique.

As leaders, we should always be motivated by love. People are not things we use to promote ourselves by providing what we need to achieve our ambitions. They aren't "checkbooks" and "Visa cards" meant to finance our aspirations. They are the "Church—the Body of Christ." They are the precious saints God has called us to serve and train in the principles of His Word. Leaders should see the offering as an opportunity for the believers to grow in faith, practice obedience, and support the Great Commission—not as an opportunity to simply "raise funds."

With regard to technique, we must take care to avoid flamboyant means that manipulate people's emotions. When we try to stir people through dramatic "prophecies" or promises of prosperity or plain embellishment, we undermine the integrity of the ministry. Paul told Titus to install leaders who are "blameless, as stewards of God...not greedy for money" (Titus 1:7). Saying that God wants people to "give an amount equal to a certain scripture reference" or that "this is a prophetic moment in which people can sow money to reap a great miracle," do the ministry a disservice. They cause people to lose respect for spiritual leaders and view them with suspicion. Saints begin to question their credibility and regard them as little more than snake oil salesmen trying to make a profit.

And is it any wonder? These ostentatious practices flow from the same spirit that pushes people over at the altar, and tells seekers to repeat certain words in an attempt to bestow the gift of tongues. It is exacting a response through manipulation. It is spiritual extortion.

A FINAL WORD

"Embezzlement" occurs when one who's been entrusted with stewardship over another's property or monies illegally uses those assets for his own selfish ends. Similarly, "Misappropriation of Funds" is to intentionally redirect designated monies (even within the organization) for uses that benefit one's personal interests. More and more often, we hear about leaders being convicted of these financial and—where the church is concerned—spiritual felonies.

It's not only the self-aggrandizing televangelists who have been charged with financial malfeasance. It's often the honest, well-intentioned leaders who are also among the accused. Their crime, however, is failing to provide due diligence in regard to reportability.

It is a grave and foolish mistake for a leader to retain sole control of an organization's finances. While some leaders feel it is an advantage to make all their own decisions about spending, it actually exposes them to temptation and undermines their credibility. People will question if money is being spent wisely and objectively. The naïve may blindly give their support, but those who are trained in ethics, or are educated professionals, will hesitate. They understand that trustworthy leadership reinforces its integrity through reportability.

Reportability is not subjecting oneself to a legalistic tribunal that scrutinizes and criticizes one's every decision. Nor is it a sign of weakness or indecisiveness that relies on a committee to run the ministry. Reportability is submitting oneself to a trusted group of individuals (e.g., board of directors, trustees, elders, etc.) who have been given the right to review. Proverbs tells us there is safety in a multitude of counselors (Proverbs 11:14). The wise leader understands this. When other individuals, such as a board or financial committee, are included in financial decisions, it provides several invaluable safeguards.

First, reportability provides wisdom in decision making. Proverbs tells us, "By wise counsel wage your war" (Proverbs 20:18). One person usually only sees one perspective of a situation. When others are consulted, the dynamics of that perspective change dramatically. Each member of the accountability group brings valuable insights that no one person can have alone. King David demonstrated this wisdom when he surrounded himself with the sons of Issachar "who understood the times to know what Israel should do" (1 Chronicles 12:32).

Second, reportability protects the leader from unwarranted suspicions. Reportability is not meant to control the leader, it is meant to shield him from indiscretions that may threaten his integrity. Some pastors, in their enthusiasm for some worthy project, may be quick to allocate funds or redirect monies to support it. Unfortunately, such eagerness often creates blind spots in which leaders lose sight of ethical concerns and accounting proprieties. Structures of accountability through regular reporting are meant to help leaders keep these concerns in view. They are not there to criticize or attack one's integrity, they are there to support and protect him.

Thirdly, reportability reinforces the integrity of the organization. Credible ministries are free of one man's control. While it is true that many successful ministries are built around the ministry or giftedness of one individual, these ministries should be structured so that the leading individual must have the support and approval of a governing board when making financial decisions. When supporters know that there are reputable individuals in place to temper decisions and establish policies, they will be more inclined to support the ministry with generous offerings.

The Barna Research Group, a marketing research company that provides analysis regarding cultural trends, revealed that tithing is down, especially in the U.S. In a recent study, one-third of Americans (34%) have dropped in the amount donated to churches and 11% say they have completely dropped all giving to churches.[8]

While George Barna, the Group's founder, did not directly connect this decline in giving to the abuses of unethical leaders, he did state that one way a church can get its people to give is to enhance its integrity and credibility. He writes, "it is helpful to give evidence of the ministry needs people's money would be devoted to, show how efficiently the church uses money, demonstrate the life-changing impact of the church's ministry, and establish trust and confidence in the leadership of the church."[9]

The Trust of Leadership

The Trust of Leadership

CHAPTER FOUR

FIDUCIARITY

Fiduciarity refers to a broad notion of financial and corporate stewardship. It implies an obligation to serve the financial interests and corporate health of those who have entrusted certain individuals with their well-being.

At the height of its success, Heritage USA was one of the top vacation destinations in the United States. It attracted nearly 6 million visitors annually and employed about 2,500 people. Founded by televangelist Jim Bakker, Heritage USA, also known as the PTL Club, had facilities that included a 500-room hotel, an indoor shopping center, a 400-unit campground, conference facilities, a skating rink, TV production studios, a Bible school, timeshares, a water park, and much, much more.

Unfortunately, what appeared to be a "Bible-themed Disneyland and Resort Center for Christians," turned out to be a cesspool of corruption and shame for the body of Christ. By the time he was forced to resign in 1987, Jim Bakker's abuse and mismanagement of the PTL Club had resulted in outstanding liens of $35 million with revenue in severe decline even as "millions continued to be siphoned off by excessive spending."[1]

Eventually Bakker was found guilty of numerous crimes, receiving a sentence of forty-five years in federal prison and a $500,000 fine.[2]

The court litigating the case commented that such a breach of fiduciary responsibility "is shocking to the conscience to the extent that it is unbelievable that a religious ministry would be operated in such a manner." The court concluded that "Mr. Bakker, as an officer and director of PTL approached the management of the corporation with reckless indifference to the financial consequences of his acts. While on the one hand he was experiencing inordinate personal gain for the revenues of PTL, on the other hand he was intentionally ignoring the extreme financial difficulties of PTL and was even adding to them. Such conduct demonstrates a total lack of fiduciary responsibility."[3]

In addition to Bakker's crimes, it was noted by the court that "trustees and corporate directors for not-for-profit organizations are liable for losses occasioned by their negligent mismanagement."[4] In fact, the main reason Heritage USA failed was not Jim Bakker, it was the failure of the board of directors to effectively fulfill their fiduciary duties. Had they fulfilled their trust of leadership, the integrity of the organization would have been preserved and, perhaps, would still remain today.

Corporate law forbids entities such as churches or nonprofits from operating without a board of directors. These directors are often called trustees because it implies that the legal and financial oversight of the church is delegated "in trust" to these individuals. State laws often require the board of directors to consist of a president (or chairman), treasurer, and secretary, as well as a minimum number of trustees or directors. The treasurer and secretary can also be directors, whereas the president does not typically vote on issues unless a tie-breaker is needed. An attorney should be consulted to verify relevant state laws.

This model for plurality in leadership is biblical. Moses realized that the task before him was beyond his single abilities. In Exodus 18, Jethro, his father-in-law observed Moses arbitrating people's concerns from morning to evening. Respectfully, Jethro rebuked Moses for trying to do too much. He counseled Moses to "select from all the people able men, such as fear God, men of truth, hating covetousness; and place such over them to be rulers of thousands, rulers of hundreds, rulers of fifties, and rulers of tens. And let them judge the people at all times" (Exodus 18:21-22). Moses followed this godly counsel which became a model for effective leadership: multiple leaders must be established to share the management of the body.

Plurality in leadership didn't stop there. It continued into the New Testament. In Acts 11:27-30, a body of elders had been formed in the Jerusalem church. Also in Acts 14, 15, 20, and 21, multiple elders are mentioned as governing bodies over local churches. Paul's preference for church leadership, as indicated in Titus 1:5, was to "appoint elders in every city" who would manage local assemblies of Christians. James said the sick should "call for the elders of the church" for prayer (James 5:14) and Peter commanded believers to submit to the elders over them (1 Peter 5:5).

It should be understood that the term "elder" did not simply mean "old person." It comes from the Greek "presbuteros" which indicates maturity in a formal leadership capacity.[5] The function of an elder was one of rule, governance, teaching, and official leadership. In both the Old and New Testaments, elders were to be above reproach who, through their integrity and character, could preserve the reputation and credibility of the church. One who "must have a good testimony among those who are outside," and can "take care of the church of God" (1 Timothy 3:5-7). In many ways, they are the forerunners of our present day boards of directors charged with maintaining the fiduciary aspects of the corporate body.

The board of directors serves three very important functions: —advisory, administrative, and accountability. In their advisory role, the collective wisdom of the board provides counsel and guidance regarding operational issues. Working together, they plan, problem solve, strategize, and offer assistance to the management team. As an administrative board, the trustees will address legal issues, review financial statements, establish policy, and fulfill portfolios relevant to each director's respective talents and abilities. The board is also a source of accountability within the organization as they provide checks and balances. Essentially, they protect the leader from himself and the organization from abuses. Lord Acton wrote, "Power corrupts and absolute power corrupts absolutely." Trustees put the leader's power in check and provide a balance when needed. By fulfilling this role as well as that of advisory and administrative, the board of directors fulfills its fiduciary duty.

THE FIDUCIARY DUTY

The term "fiduciarity" refers to a broad notion of financial and corporate stewardship. It implies an "obligation to serve the financial interests (and corporate health) of those who have entrusted certain individuals with their well-being."[6] It comes from the word "fiduciary" which comes from the Latin "fiducia," meaning "trust." A fiduciary is a person who has been entrusted with the power and authority to act for another under circumstances which require total trust, good faith, and honesty. It is from this concept that we derive the term "trustee." The trustee, or one who has been entrusted, is responsible to ensure the trustworthiness of the organization. His authority is given, not to serve his own interests, or the interests of certain privileged individuals, his role is to preserve the integrity of the organization and guard the interests of those who are relying on him.

If your friend went on a trip and left you to care for his dog, you would be your friend's fiduciary in the matter of his dog's well-being. You would be holding that dog "in trust" until your friend returns. Undoubtedly, you would keep the dog safe in your care, provide it with food and water and even walk the dog when it needed exercise. As a faithful fiduciary, you would render all due diligence toward that animal because you know that if any harm came to it, you would be blamed for its demise. The good news is, you wouldn't be held responsible (or liable) for its harm unless you somehow violated your duties to care for the dog (didn't feed or water it, let it play in traffic). If you did all your due diligence, your friend might be mad at you, but he cannot hold you liable.

Being a member of a board of directors, or a trustee, over a certain entity is the same thing. You are given fiduciary responsibility over that body and it is up to you to exercise all due diligence to ensure that it remains healthy. If the entity fails you may become unpopular, but you cannot be held liable unless that failure was a direct result of your own breach of fiduciary trust. Jim Bakker was held liable because he "let the dog die." He failed to properly care for the entity entrusted to him.

Likewise, when trustees fail to exercise their responsibility as fiduciary agents, they put themselves at risk. In fact, what occurred in 1988 at Heritage USA has resulted in a shift regarding liability of corporate officers. Traditionally, the officers and directors of nonprofits had little or no risk of personal legal liability, but since the PTL debacle, numerous lawsuits have attempted—with some success—to incur legal and financial penalties on corporate directors who have been found in breach of their fiduciary duties.

BOARD LIABILITY

A study entitled "Wrongdoing by Officers and Directors of Charities" researched incidents involving criminal and civil wrongdoing by officers and directors of charitable organizations between 1995 and 2002. Of the 152 incidents found through newspaper reports, 104 involved criminal activity and 54 involved breaches of fiduciary duties (6 involved both).

Of the 104 charged with crimes, 11 trustees (directors), 88 presidents (CEOs), and 10 treasurers were prosecuted and convicted. Of this grouping, 74 went to jail and 46 were imposed with restitution penalties of over $30 million, collectively. Of the 54 incidents involving breaches of fiduciary duty, 27 trustees, 44 presidents, and 2 treasurers were either removed, forced to resign, punitively fined, or forced to pay restitution of over $106 million, collectively.[7]

Richard R. Hammer, in his volume, *Pastor, Church and Law*, lists eight theories of liability for board members and corporate officers. These reflect the most common incidents of litigation resulting from trustees' dereliction of duty.[8]

"Board members may be personally liable for their own torts (conduct causing personal injury to another). This includes negligence to supervise church activities, knowingly permitting an unsafe condition to exist, uttering defamatory remarks about individuals, knowingly writing checks against insufficient funds, knowingly making false representations of the finances of the organization, etc."

"Board members may be personally liable for contracts they sign if they do so without authorization, or if they fail to indicate they are signing as a representation of the organization."

"Board members have a fiduciary duty to use reasonable care in the discharge of their duties, and they may be personally liable for damages resulting for their failure to do so. He must serve in "good faith" in the manner he believes to be in the best interest of the corporation and with such care as an ordinary prudent person in a like position would use under similar circumstances. Good faith requires the undivided loyalty of a corporate director or officer to the corporation, and such a duty of loyalty prohibits the director from using this position of trust for his own personal gain to the detriment of the corporation."

"Board members have a fiduciary duty of loyalty to the organization, and they may be personally liable for breaching this duty by participating in board decisions that place the interests of one or more board members above the interests of the church itself." This is known as "self-dealing." It is when a board member uses his influence as a fiduciary to promote deals for his own personal benefit, or the benefits of friends.

"Board members may be personally liable for diverting designated funds or trust funds to some other purpose."

"Federal and state securities laws make board members personally liable for acts of fraud committed by an organization in connection with the offer or sale of securities. These laws apply to churches and, as a result, church board members may be liable for fraudulent practices occurring in connection with the offer or sale of church securities."

"Board members may be personally liable if they participate in a decision to terminate an employee in a way that violates the employee's legal rights."

"Board members who have authority to sign checks or make financial decisions may be personally liable for a willful failure to withhold federal payroll taxes, or to deposit or pay over withheld taxes to the IRS."

Indeed serving as a board member is a great honor, but there is more at stake than simply having an important title. Board members have serious responsibilities that legally bind them to the activities of the organization. If they do not fulfill their fiduciary duties, they can and often will be held liable.

BOARD RESONSIBILITIES

It is a long established principle of corporate law that the business and affairs of a corporation are to be conducted by, and exercised under, the direction of a board of directors. In order for an entity to maintain its "trust" as honest, credible, and trustworthy, the directors must act (1) in good faith, (2) in a manner that is in the best interest of the corporation, (3) which requires making reasonable inquiry when appropriate, and (4) just as an ordinarily prudent person would do in a similar position and under similar circumstances.

This means the directors should make themselves reasonably informed in matters that come before the board. They must actively participate in decisions of the board, ask questions and propose additional information or investigation when necessary. They must act honestly, carefully and cautiously before making decisions. This does not mean they will understand every technical detail about a matter, but they should engage in the discussions to encourage thoughtful deliberations that promote the best course of action for the organization. The following are a few specifics that will help trustees to become effective fiduciaries:

Attend meetings regularly. Attendance at meetings is a must. If you cannot attend meetings, you cannot be entrusted as a fiduciary. A director must be informed and aware. And the only way to be aware is to attend meetings where discussion, interaction, and even when disagreement, occurs. You need to be there to vote and provide input. Failure to attend does not remove liability, it demonstrates dereliction of duty.

Thoroughly review financials. All interim and annual financial statements must be examined and understood. Do not be reluctant to ask questions. If you don't understand a cash flow report, a profit and loss statement, or a balance sheet, ask for clarification. This is a primary function of a trustee, if you don't seek to understand, you have failed in your duty.

Take minutes. The "minutes" are the written record of the board's deliberations and decisions while in session. According to the Evangelical Council for Financial Accountability (ECFA), minutes should contain the following components: a list of board members present as well as those absent; the meeting's location, start time, and ending time; a record of actions taken by the board with enough discussion to substantiate the actions taken; and the abstention of interested parties when necessary.[9]

Avoid haste in making decisions. A director should make decisions only after being fully briefed on the issues being impacted by the decision. If more information is needed, request it. If more time is required, ask for it. Be wary of haste in decisions because it often indicates that something is being "pushed" through by keeping directors uninformed. As well, be careful of important items that are presented late in the meeting, after everyone has grown tired and wants to finish quickly and adjourn. Chairmen who intentionally do this demonstrate a lack of integrity by manipulating the board.

Prepare. Courts have been particularly critical of directors who do not avail themselves of all material information pertinent to the matter on which they are asked to vote. If the director feels the information being provided is inadequate, he should point that out and require more data before a decision is made.

Ask questions. A director should probe, test, and judge the reliability and accuracy of information being presented. Don't assume everything is correct—think critically. Even more important, as a board member, don't ever, ever be a "Yes Man." As was stated by the court in the Jim Bakker case, "The law has no place for dummy directors."

Investigate all questionable or suspicious issues. The director exists to protect the fiduciary interests of the organization. If there are matters that seem suspicious, unfair, or unethical, he has an obligation to bring those issues to the table and address them with the board.

Become familiar with corporate documents. Directors have a responsibility to uphold the bylaws of the corporation. Rather than relying on others to provide such information or relate their interpretation, directors should seek their own understanding of corporate documents.

Register objections. There may be serious issues that leave you with unresolved concerns. In order to protect yourself from liability, you may need to voice your dissent from board actions, and have your objection registered in the minutes.

Tender resignation. The above issues enable directors to perform their duties effectively, with due diligence, and fiduciary excellence. Directors who are aware of their inability to do so, and are unable to improve their efforts, should resign.

Serving as a corporate director is a serious duty. The director should see himself as a servant to the people who are the constituency of the organization. Failure to fulfill the above responsibilities is a failure to serve the people who put you in that office.

BOARD GUIDELINES

In an organization, the board's authority is not absolute. There are certain parameters that limit how and when they exercise their fiduciary duties. It is important to understand these so as not to overstep boundaries. By the same token, there are certain responsibilities a director has that are often portrayed as presumptuous, disrespectful or even rebellious. The following are some common issues boards must navigate as they seek to be effective fiduciary managers.

The authority of the board of directors exists only as a board at a legal meeting. The fiduciary authority to manage the organization is vested upon the directors only when called to order, at an official meeting, with a quorum being present. No individual director carries legal authority by himself. In other words, he does not have the right to make decisions, give commands, or initiate actions on his own initiative—his authority exists only as he is a part of the board. Nor does any minority or majority of board members carry authority at an informal, private meeting. Unless a formal meeting is called and all members have been informed of the meeting as stipulated in the bylaws, their action is not binding upon the corporation. The reason for this is obvious. "The law believes that the greatest wisdom results from conference and exchange of individual views, and it is for this reason that the law requires the united wisdom of a majority of the members of the board in determining the business of the corporation."[10]

A meeting of the board of directors is not legal unless a quorum is present. A quorum refers to a percentage of directors that must be present in order for the board to transact business. The quorum is typically defined in the bylaws. If not, a majority of board members usually constitutes a quorum. Requiring a quorum prevents a minority of board members from making significant decisions that affect the health of the organization.

Loyalty is to the organization, not the leader. Richard R. Hammer states, "Board members have a fiduciary duty of loyalty to the organization, and they may be personally liable for breaching this duty by participating in board decisions that place the interests of one or more board members above the interests of the church itself." The trustees' first loyalty is to the health of the organization, not the individual who leads it or any other person in the room. There will be times when directors must raise their voices in disagreement. Hammer goes on to state that there may even be extreme instances when one's objection should be noted in the minutes. This applies to issues that the trustee may feel is a breach of fiduciary responsibility.

Disagreement is not always rebellion. Submission to authority is a virtue that sincere Christ followers try to emulate. Submitting to authority, however, does not mean one can never disagree with his authority. In fact, those who are legally vested with fiduciary roles are expected to disagree with authority for the sake of the body. A healthy board is made up of people who are critical thinkers and unafraid to speak their minds. "Yes Men" are worthless in the boardroom. They bring no value to the discussion and undermine the fiduciary excellence of the team.

Directors must be free to share their views. There should be no firewall between directors who share a common, fiduciary responsibility. No appointment to a subcommittee, no membership on a task force or implied confidentiality regarding corporate matters should prevent any trustee from openly sharing his opinion at a legal meeting of the corporate officers. Again, corporate "law believes that the greatest wisdom results from conference and exchange of individual views, and it is for this reason that the law requires the united wisdom of a majority of the members of the board in determining the business of the corporation." Any attempt to shut down this open and free discourse will disable the fiduciary responsibility of the board and expose the directors to risk.

Unity should prevail after the vote. While we want directors who are strong enough to speak their minds, we also want them to be meek enough to submit after the vote is taken, especially if they don't get their way. As noted above, there will be times when a trustee must break rank and register his objection, but that is in extreme situations where a breach of fiduciary duty is concerned. Most of the time, decisions are more about planning and policy and do not rise to such a critical level. When directors exit the board meeting, they should not conduct secret meetings to build a consensus among the constituency against the board and in favor of their particular opinion. The place for this is in the board room. What happens in the board room, stays in the board room (unless it is a breach of fiduciary duty).

Seek to foster an atmosphere of encouragement. Being the leader is difficult. There is a constant stream of voices, both internal and external, tearing at the leader's confidence. Internally, whispers of insecurity, fear and self-condemnation constantly assail the leader's mind and cause him to question his call. Externally, the critics can be relentless. Almost everyone has an opinion about the way things should be. Add to this the vicious assaults of the enemy who constantly hurls fiery darts against the leader, tearing him down. Directors need to realize they have a responsibility, not only to the fiduciary interests of the organization, but also to the effectiveness of the leader. Just as Aaron and Hur held up the arms of Moses, directors are there to support the leader, hold his arms and encourage his resolve. Speak words of life and hope into your leader. Pray for him and *tell* him you're praying for him. Speak in support of his vision whenever you can and guard him from voices of gossip, slander, and dissent.

The Trust of Leadership

A FINAL WORD

Some board members struggle over what appears to be a conflict of loyalty. On the one hand they want to effectively serve the organization and its constituency, while on the other hand they want to serve and be loyal to the leader (CEO, pastor, chairman, owner). At some point every director will find himself in this position where it seems the two loyalties conflict, but in reality they do not.

Having served as a trustee on numerous boards, I have often been confronted with this dilemma. I recall an instance where my leader had a vision with which I disagreed. I felt it was too costly, required too much time and energy, and did not serve the core values of the organization. For me to disagree with him was not an act of disloyalty—on the contrary, it was the best way I could serve him.

If I agreed simply out of a desire to be supportive, I would be depriving him of a perspective he may need to see. By disagreeing, or challenging him, it allows him to encounter concerns or issues that may eventually become an obstacle to embarrass or undermine him. Essentially, the more concern I raise, the more concern I am showing for my leader. Sadly, the downfall of some leaders is that they would rather be ruined by praise than perfected by criticism. They disable a free exchange of ideas, cause board members to feel guilty for raising objections, and refuse the collective wisdom God is trying to give them.

Having said that, directors must always be careful not to confuse the limitations of their role. The director is not the CEO, the deacon is not the pastor, and the trustee is not the chairman of the board. It is healthy to raise objections, but one must always know the limits of his authority. I have known board members who mistakenly believed their vision was just as important as the pastor's vision and, in fact, tried to implement their vision over that of the pastor's. This is called "Leading from Behind" and it is a subtle form of rebellion. Always remember, while you are there to guard the fiduciary interests of the organization, you are also there to promote the vision that God has given the leader and propel him forward. The exception lies only in situations where fiduciary responsibilities are being breached.

The Trust of Leadership

The Trust of Leadership

CHAPTER FIVE

HUMILITY

C.S. Lewis famously said, "True humility is not thinking less of yourself; it is thinking of yourself less." Nowhere is this truth more demonstrated than in the realm of leadership.

A kleptocracy is a corrupt government that enlarges the personal wealth and power of government officials at the expense of the population and national interests.

Mobutu Sésé Seko, was the President of Zaire (now the Democratic Republic of the Congo) for 32 years (1965–97). While in office, Mobutu worked mostly on increasing his personal fortune, which in 1984 was estimated to amount to $5 billion. This was almost equivalent to the country's foreign debt at the time, forcing the Zaire government to default on loans from Belgium in 1989. Despite the nation's failing economy, Mobutu chartered a Concorde aircraft for his international travel and owned a fleet of Mercedes-Benz vehicles that he used to travel between his numerous palaces. During his leadership, the nation's roads rotted, infrastructure virtually collapsed, state employees went months without being paid, and many of his people starved. Meanwhile, most of the nation's financial resources were siphoned off to Mobutu, his family, and top government officials earning him a reputation as one of the world's foremost examples of kleptocracy and corruption.

In 1979, when Nigeria had oil revenues reaching $24 billion per year, President Alhaji Shehu Shagari's administration was termed "a government of contractors, for contractors and by contractors." Meetings of cabinet members and party leaders were reputed to be "grand bazaars where the resources of the state were put up for auction" and kickbacks to government officials for awarding contracts rose to 50 percent. Even after the oil boom came to an end and the economy was on the verge of collapse, politicians continued to bribe, steal, smuggle and accumulate vast fortunes while schools, civil projects and hospitals went bankrupt.[1]

In Zimbabwe, President Robert Mugabe built a palace fit for a king. The cost of the project is estimated at $10,000,000 in a country where factory workers earn as little as $10 per month, unemployment is at 85 percent, hyperinflation is estimated at 6.5 sextillion percent[2] and 5.5 million people (almost half the population) are in need of hunger relief.[3] As described in a recent report by Physicians for Human Rights, the Mugabe regime destroyed the country's healthcare system and enacted policies that ruined what had been a vibrant agriculture—depriving all but a tiny elite of proper nutrition, water, and a sustainable livelihood. The results of Mugabe's leadership include a cholera epidemic, rampant diseases, and a life expectancy that fell from 62 years in 1990 to 36 in 2006.

"The trouble with Nigeria," wrote the Nigerian novelist Chinua Achebe in 1983, "is simply and squarely a failure of leadership. There is nothing basically wrong with the Nigerian character. There is nothing wrong with the Nigerian land or climate or water or air or anything else. The Nigerian problem is the unwillingness or inability of its leaders to rise to the responsibility, to the challenge of personal example which are the hallmarks of true leadership."[4]

Although writing specifically about his own homeland, Achebe was describing the underlying cancer that corrupts leadership regardless of tribe, tongue or nation—the leader's lust for enlargement. Whether it is an African dictator, an American CEO or a Communist despot, one's egregious abuse of authority demonstrates the underlying trait of every corrupt leader. They come to view leadership as a means to serve themselves rather than the people they are called to serve. They regard their followers as things to use to better their own lives, rather than using their position to better the lives of others.

THE MIND OF CHRIST

C.S. Lewis famously said, "True humility is not thinking less of yourself; it is thinking of yourself less." Nowhere is this truth more demonstrated than in the realm of leadership.

The Apostle Paul wrote: "Let this mind be in you which was also in Christ Jesus, who, being in the form of God, did not consider it robbery to be equal with God, but made Himself of no reputation, taking the form of a bondservant, and coming in the likeness of men. And being found in appearance as a man, He humbled Himself and became obedient to the point of death, even the death of the cross" (Philippians 2:5-8).

If anyone was entitled to lord authority, power, and privilege over people, it was Jesus Christ. He was the Creator, the highest authority, the Eternal Son of God Whom heaven and earth will worship for all eternity. But Jesus did not come demanding that we serve Him, He came to serve us. He did not come with a scepter of authority, expecting us to lay down our lives to aggrandize His life. On the contrary—He laid down His life in order to offer us life, and life more abundantly.

This was the example of leadership Jesus imparted to His followers.

In Mark 10:37, James and John said to Jesus, "Grant us that we may sit, one on Your right hand and the other on Your left, in Your glory." They had it all wrong. They thought leadership was about getting authority and being in control. For them, leadership was about privilege and prestige. It was a means to gain power and control over the ones they were leading.

This is how most people think of leadership. To them, being a great leader is having a great reputation that enjoys prestige, privilege, and respect. But Jesus had a different idea about great leadership. He said, "...whoever desires to become great among you shall be your servant...And whoever of you desires to be first shall be slave of all" (Mark 10:43-44). To Jesus, leadership was servanthood and the greatest leaders were those who acted like servants.

What does it mean to be a servant? It means to give yourself in the service of others. A servant is concerned more with meeting the needs of those he serves, than he is with his own needs. James and John, however, were caught up in a worldly attitude regarding leadership. They thought being a leader was about advancing and promoting themselves. To them, it centered on being admired, gaining authority and exercising control over others. Even worse, to the worldly thinker, leadership is a means of holding others down and using them to fulfill your own personal ambitions.

But in Christ, leadership is the exact opposite. Consider Jesus' response to James and John. "You know that those who are considered rulers over the Gentiles lord it over them, and their great ones exercise authority over them. Yet it shall not be so among you...whoever desires to become great among you shall be your servant and whoever of you desires to be first shall be slave of all." According to Christ, leadership is not promoting or advancing self; neither is it holding others down to serve you. In Christ, leadership is being more concerned with the needs and welfare of others than you are with your own. We lead, not to be admired, honored or recognized, but out of a love for others. We seek positions only to edify and meet the needs of others, to lift others and better their positions.

The image of Jesus Christ, Second Person of the Eternal Trinity, stooping down with towel and basin to scrub the filth-stained feet of the disciples is astounding. It shows us that authority given by God to a leader is means to serve. Herein lies the trust of leadership. Those in positions of leadership have been trusted with authority, not to serve or enlarge themselves, but to enlarge the organization and serve the ones they are leading. It is when the leader—who has been empowered with the right to initiate action, give commands and cast vision—puts the needs of the people before the needs of himself.

Such a feat cannot be accomplished without humility. As seen in Christ, humility is the ability to set aside rights and privilege, to demote yourself and make others the priority—to think of yourself less. Jesus came with no pretense of elevation. His only concern was to fully give Himself, to sacrifice Himself on a cross, so others might live. This is what makes leaders great—not the ability to merely achieve great things, but the ability to achieve great things for the benefit of others.

Consider these words from Nelson Mandela, former president of South Africa. "During my lifetime I have dedicated myself to the struggle of the African people. I have fought against white domination, and I have fought against black domination. I have cherished the ideal of a democratic and free society in which all persons live together in harmony and with equal opportunities."[5] Because of his commitment to serve his people, Mandala (after 26 years in prison) became the first black president of South Africa, defeated "apartheid," earned the Nobel Peace Prize and to this day remains one of the world's most admired political leaders. Mandela models the essence of good leadership. Rather than using his position to seize control of the nation, destroy his opposition, give positions to all his friends, and amass wealth to himself, he remained committed to his principles. He never faltered from working toward democracy and prosperity for all.

Léopold Senghor became president of Senegal in 1960. Prior to his presidency, he studied theology at Catholic Seminary. While there he pressed for better living conditions for the students and was turned down for the priesthood because his insistent advocacy for their needs was perceived as a lack of a "spirit of obedience."⁶ It was this compassion for his fellow man that made him one of the most beloved leaders in African history. Throughout his political career, he demonstrated a respect toward others and resisted the totalitarian excesses of other West African leaders. Although Senegal was a one-party political system, Senghor introduced amendments to the constitution to foster multiparty politics. In fact, in 1981, he resigned the presidency and promoted his prime minister, becoming the first leader of an independent African country to give up power voluntarily. Senghor is one of the few leaders to ever demonstrate the essence of biblical leadership: to prefer others over yourself.

Tanzania elected its first president after achieving independence from Britain in 1961. It was a revolution won not with bullets or bloodshed, but through the impressive leadership of soon-to-be president, Julius Nyerere. While some may debate his political idealism or socialistic programs, one thing about him has never been questioned: the depth and sincerity of his humility.

When Nyerere became head of state, he was so popular that he could have easily elevated himself as a king or dictator. Others around him were doing it. Amin, Mugabe, and Mobutu rose in power only to use it as a way to crush opposition, fortify their authority, and amass wealth for their friends and families. But Nyerere did exactly the opposite. He chose to live the modest example of putting one's community before one's own interests.

For example, shortly after taking office, he cut the salaries of all government ministers by 20-50 percent, including his own. Although by world standards these ministers were poorly paid, by Tanzanian standards they were very rich. Nyerere argued that a poor country, such as theirs, should not have leaders who lived luxuriously. Many government leaders opposed the cuts and resigned their positions, but Nyerere remained firm in his ideals.

He was a devout Catholic known for his frequent fasting and his disavowal of pomp and privilege. He never received more than

$8,000 a year as President and dressed modestly in a gray or black safari shirt over his trousers and a white crocheted skullcap. In contrast to many African leaders, who often raced through their capitals in convoys of Mercedes Benzes with armies of police in motorcycle escort, Nyerere moved around Dar es Salaam in an old car with just his driver, who stopped for red lights.

Rather than coveting more and more power, Nyerere retired as head of state in 1985 and took on the role of diplomat and peacemaker. Because he was so trusted, he was invited to mediate disputes all across the African continent and worked alongside Nelson Mandela to put an end to apartheid in South Africa. Even the Catholic Church admired his integrity so much that, in 2005, he was proposed for beatification—which is one step away from sainthood.

MOTIVATION

There are two types of motivations that drive leaders. As seen by Mobutu and Mugabe, there are leaders who are driven by selfish ambition, and there are leaders like Nyerere and Mandela who are motivated by a love for others. The former are much like James and John; they are concerned primarily about personal elevation and act out of self-interest. The latter, like Christ, are more interested in serving, edifying, and accomplishing good for the benefit of others. This truth is not some ethereal idealism. It is based upon practical examples demonstrated in the life of the ultimate servant-leader, Jesus Christ.

First, the servant-leader has an awareness of his accountability to God. Jesus said, "The Son of Man can do nothing of Himself, but what He sees the Father do; for whatever He does, the Son also does in like manner" (John 5:19). In other words, the servant-leader realizes he must pattern his leadership after God. He knows that God has set the standard for right and wrong and he will ultimately answer to God for his conduct, especially as a leader.

This was the point of the story told by Jesus in Luke 12:42-48. "And the Lord said, "Who then is that faithful and wise steward, whom his master will make ruler over his household, to give them their portion of food in due season? Blessed is that servant whom his master will find so doing when he comes. Truly, I say to you that he will make him ruler over all that he has. But if that servant says in his heart, 'My master is delaying his coming,' and begins to beat the male and female servants, and to eat and drink and be drunk, the master of that servant will come on a day when he is not looking for him, and at an hour when he is not aware, and will cut him in two and appoint him his portion with the unbelievers. And that servant who knew his master's will, and did not prepare himself or do according to his will, shall be beaten with many stripes. But he who did not know, yet committed things deserving of stripes, shall be beaten with few. For everyone to whom much is given, from him much will be required; and to whom much has been committed, of him they will ask the more." Jesus made it clear that leaders, because of their scope of authority, who have more influence, more control, more decision-making capacity, will be held into account on a much broader spectrum than those who were not commissioned as leaders.

Similarly, James 3:1 says, "My brethren, let not many of you become teachers, knowing that we shall receive a stricter judgment." Those who are called to stand before others to instruct, cast vision and lead will be held to a harsher, stricter standard of judgment. This truth is indicated in Romans 13:1 where authority is portrayed as being given to leaders from God, who expects them to act with justice and equity.

Paul also reminds us in 1 Corinthians 4:2, "Moreover it is required in stewards that one be found faithful." A steward is one who is charged with managing the affairs of another. This is exactly the work of leadership. Authority has been established by God and handed to men that they may administer his care and benevolence to mankind. Those who fail to do so by abusing their authority will be held accountable at the day of their judgment as stated in Hebrews 9:27, "It is appointed for men to die once, but after this the judgment."

Someone once asked the great scholar, Daniel Webster, "You have a colossal mind. What is the greatest thought that you have ever had?" He replied, "I've thought about many things, but the most awesome, the most terrifying, the most shattering thought I've ever had is my personal accountability to God one day."[7] If every politician, every leader, every pastor, CEO, and manager conducted their affairs with this truth in mind, corruption and the abuse of authority would practically vanish from the earth.

Unfortunately, the carnal leader, driven by selfish ambition, disregards his accountability to God. It's not that he won't be accountable, it's that he discards concern for it. He pretends away the notion that one day he will die and stand before the King from Whom all authority flows and chooses only to believe that in this life there is punishment and reward. So, in this life he uses his authority to reward himself with all his power can grasp. He amasses wealth, he enlarges control, he takes from others, and destroys all who oppose. His motivation is only for himself and what makes his own life richer and more powerful. But despite what the egotistical leader believes, eternity begins with accountability. All power, all authority will bow before God and be held accountable for the evil, or the good, they did with the influence God had given them.

Those that are humble acknowledge this accountability to God. But those who are proud see themselves as the highest authority and care only for what best serves them.

Secondly, the servant-leader recognizes the worth and value of every soul. This was what motivated Jesus. In Luke 15:4-6, He told the parable of a man who had a hundred sheep. After realizing that one lamb was lost, the man left the ninety-nine and searched after the missing lamb until he found it. Just as the one lost lamb held significance to the shepherd, so does every individual life have incredible value to God. Nowhere was this demonstrated more than on the cross. Romans 5:8 tells us, "God demonstrates His own love toward us, in that while we were still sinners, Christ died for us." The cross is the revelation of the love of God for the human soul. For every person, God has a plan. For every life, God has a purpose. Jeremiah 29:11 reveals this: "For I know the thoughts that I think toward you, says the Lord, thoughts of peace and not of evil, to give you a future and a hope."

For the servant-leader, modeled after Christ, this is the motivation for his service. He leads, acutely aware of the value of each person under his charge. Decisions are made, actions are taken with regard for how the lives of people will be impacted. Will people be lifted up or taken down? How will the lives of people be made better or caused to suffer? He sees himself as a servant of people, enacting programs, initiating action so as to help and improve the life of each individual lamb.

By contrast, the carnal, self-absorbed leader sees people as things to use, not to serve. While he may recognize the worth of people, their value relates only to how it serves his interests. He is not concerned about promoting them and helping to achieve a better condition, he is concerned about his own condition and how they can be used to better it.

King Ahab ruled the northern kingdom of Israel in 1 Kings 21. Nearby lived Naboth, a citizen who owned a coveted parcel of property next to the king's palace. It was a lush, fertile field that provided its owner with rich, fruitful vineyards over the years, and King Ahab wanted it for himself. First, the king tried to intimidate Naboth into surrendering it. When that failed, he offered him money. Still, Naboth refused to relinquish his family's ancestral property, a right which was provided to him under Mosaic Law (Numbers 36:7-9).

King Ahab, however, had little regard for what was "right" and even less regard for Naboth. He consented to a malicious plot in which Naboth would be falsely accused of treason and murdered. As a result, his coveted property could be justifiably seized by the state and with the stroke of a quill, Ahab would have a new garden. It is a biblical paragon of how the powerful take advantage of the weak in order to add to their power, wealth, and position.

Perhaps the saddest irony in this story is that the king had a solemn responsibility to protect the rights of his citizens as defined by Mosaic Law (Deuteronomy 17:14-20). Ahab should have defended Naboth; he should have taken up his cause and pleaded for his deliverance. Instead, he took advantage of the power differential afforded by his title and leveraged his position to serve his own interests—all at Naboth's expense. Ahab's authority became corrupt.

Pride is the condition of exaggerating one's own worth or sense of importance. For leaders, it is a feeling of superiority over those we lead.

There's a subtle danger that comes with being a leader. It is the feeling that, because I have the position—because I am the one in authority with the title, the vision, and the command over others—I am more important than everyone else. I matter more. My gifts, my talents, my expertise makes me superior and more valuable. It is this arrogance that causes leaders to hold others in low esteem and use them as objects to serve the leader's ambition.

It's the business manager who demands more hours from an employee with little regard for her personal sacrifice and struggle. It's the pastor who manipulates excessive donations from congregants who can barely afford food for their children. It's the politician who thinks of people in terms of votes needed to win the next election rather than citizens whose rights need to be protected.

If we aspire to leadership out of a desire for power, recognition or control, we are aspiring for the wrong reason. Our leadership will be polluted with impure motives and corrupted by carnal ambition. What's worse is it will be void of God's blessing and will actually draw down His curse. James 4:6 says, "God resists the proud." Proverbs 16:18 tell us that "Pride goes before destruction, and a haughty spirit before a fall." Self-promotion provokes God to move against us and pull us down. Humility, on the other hand, invokes God's blessing and rich provision.

Thirdly, the servant-leader is focused on the long term good he can achieve for others. The self-centered leader cares only about immediate, self-aggrandizing gratification. In fact, great servant-leaders exhaust their lives building a vision that will outlast themselves. Consider the difference between Jesus and the Pharisees, the religious leaders of His day.

Jesus said, "No man takes my life, I lay it down Myself" (John 10:18). He was referring to the cross upon which He would offer His perfect, sinless life as an atonement for the sins of men. Hebrews 12:2 says that Jesus, "...for the joy that was set before Him endured the cross, despising the shame." He endured the cross because He was focused on the good He would achieve for others, the long term and eternal good. It wasn't the nails that held Him there, it was His love for mankind. It wasn't the Romans or the Jews that took His life—He gave it. He could have obliterated them all with a mere spoken word. No, the cross didn't hold Him, He held the cross. He stretched out His arms and embraced a death that would satisfy the justice of God meant for the sins of the world. His sacrificed paved the way for humanity's return to God.

By contrast, the Pharisees had no regard for the people, the nation, or even God. Their only concern was political expedience. They lusted after power and control "...and killed the Prince of life!" (Acts 3:15). This is the mark of a selfish leader—there's no vision for the future, there's no strategy for improving people's lives. There's only the next election cycle and what keeps them in power. In the words of James Freeman Clarke, "The difference between a politician and a statesman is: a politician thinks of the next election and a statesman thinks of the next generation."

Statesmen are leaders who use their influence and authority to build lasting, sustainable institutions that serve the good of mankind. They are willing to be unpopular for the greater good. They

The Trust of Leadership

are willing to say things that are offensive and stand for what others may despise because it is exactly what needs to change.

Known as the "Master Builder," Robert Moses is credited by many as the visionary who made possible the culturally and economically vibrant New York City we know today. Others have a less romantic view: they say he loved cars and hated people.

In the dawn of the automobile age, Robert Moses foresaw an age where the automobile would overcome mass transit. It was his vision that built vehicular bridges, tunnels, and roadways that transformed the city into a network of highways allowing the free-flow of goods, services, and people across the five boroughs, Long Island, and upstate New York. While many criticize him for the destruction of neighborhoods, and disregard for the thousands of residents displaced by his bulldoze-and-build philosophy, the sheer breadth of his achievements is astonishing. His accomplishments from 1924 to 1968 include Lincoln Center, Jones Beach, Shea Stadium, the Central Park Zoo, 658 playgrounds, 13 bridges, 10 giant swimming pools, 416 miles of parkways, towers with 28,400 new apartments, and more than two million acres of parks in the city and surrounding regions, and across New York State.

No politician could have accomplished what this leader has done. It was too painful, too controversial, and too politically dangerous. Moses endured incredible criticism by opponents of his projects. Entire neighborhoods were demolished, hundreds of small businesses relocated, thousands of families displaced. At times, he was the most hated man in the city.

What drove him? What compelled him? Ambition? Glory? No, what drove him was his awareness of what New York City needed. What compelled him was a focus on the long term good he knew he could achieve for others. He knew the city would be choked as population increased and the automobile became more popular. He knew that infrastructure was not keeping pace with demands of modern society. So, he set out with a vision to build a city, not for the present masses, but for a future generation. He built the New York City we know and need today.

This is what credible, trustworthy leadership does. True leaders do not seek the immediate gratification that comes from popularity and applause—true leaders look to the future and drive people forward. In the words of Rosalynn Carter: "A great leader takes people where they don't necessarily want to go, but ought to be." True, trustworthy leadership seeks to understand what people need, not just now but in the future. It understands where the people "ought to be" and pulls them there by force and power of its passion.

In 2008, we began raising funds for our building project. As lead pastor, I knew that our building and grounds would continue to deteriorate and we would soon outgrow our facilities. It was a $3.4 million project that included new site work, a new school, and enlargement of our main worship facility. Unfortunately, 2008 was also the year the American economy collapsed. The housing bubble burst, millions lost their jobs, income and wages took a dive and donations to non-profits were at an all-time low. There were critics, dissenters, complainers, and cynics. I was accused of caring more about buildings than people. I was told that we should give our money to the poor. Some people left the church. Others refused to support. But, thankfully, the overwhelming majority saw the vision I had. We needed to build if we were to have a sustainable future. I led the people forward to the place I knew they "ought to be" and by God's grace, the building project is now completed, the people are rejoicing and the church is growing in record numbers. Had I taken the easy road to preserve my popularity and enjoy the applause of a challenge-less, changeless, stagnant vision, we would still be in that place of decay and decline.

Trust in leadership occurs when it rises from the desire to better the lives of others. But leaders who seek the immediate gratification of affirmation and applause are weak and incompetent. They're not leaders, they're politicians seeking to win elections.

A FINAL WORD

The presence of humility in the life of the leader is demonstrated by "servant-leadership."

The phrase "servant leadership" was coined by Robert K. Greenleaf in *The Servant as Leader*—an essay he published in 1970.[8] In that essay, Greenleaf wrote, "The servant-leader *is* servant first… It begins with the natural feeling that one wants to serve, to serve *first*. Then conscious choice brings one to aspire to lead. That person is sharply different from one who is *leader* first, perhaps because of the need to assuage an unusual power drive or to acquire material possessions…The leader-first and the servant-first are two extreme types."

Greenleaf further wrote, "The difference manifests itself in the care taken by the servant-first to make sure that other people's highest priority needs are being served. The best test, and difficult to administer, is: Do those served grow as persons? Do they, *while being served,* become healthier, wiser, freer, more autonomous, more likely themselves to become servants? *And,* what is the effect on the least privileged in society? Will they benefit or at least not be further deprived?"

Taking our example from Jesus Christ, a servant-leader primarily focuses on the well-being of people and the communities to which they belong. While carnal, self-centered leadership pursues the accumulation power, servant leadership is different. The servant-leader shares power, puts the needs of others first and helps people develop and perform as highly as possible.

This is the humility of leadership. It is the lowering of one's own self and giving preference to others. It is caring about others more than I care about myself. It is building a vision that is more important than my popularity—a vision that will outlast my life. This is the rock of leadership. This is the trust of leadership: I lead, not for my own benefit, but for the benefit of others.

The Trust of Leadership

CHAPTER SIX

COLLEGIALITY

Collegiality is the cooperative relationship of colleagues working together. Specifically, it is an organizational culture where collaboration and mutual accountability exists between leaders.

Sir Ernest Shackleton was a British explorer and captain of the famed ship, *Endurance*, who made the first attempt to lead a crew of men across the Antarctic. Tragically, in November of 1915, Shackleton's ship sank, leaving the crew of 27 men stranded on floating ice with minimal supplies and a few small lifeboats. The mission to cross the Antarctic was never achieved, however, their survival in the frigid, life-threatening conditions would be listed among the greatest archetypes of leadership known to man. Because Shackleton was able to keep all his men alive for two years until he could bring them home, he became known as "the greatest leader that ever came on God's earth, bar none."

The key to Shackleton's survival and success, however, was not simply his own brilliance as a leader, it was also a product of the culture he had created as a leader.[1,2,3]

It was a culture of unyielding optimism in which he always expressed his absolute confidence that every man would survive and be rescued. It was a culture of cooperation and mutual sacrifice among the men which Shackleton was first to demonstrate. When telling his men they needed to leave behind personal items to lighten their load, he was first to lay down a Bible given to him by Queen Alexandra in the snow and walk away. It was a culture of trust and friendship which he was first to model. In addition to developing personal friendships with each crewmember, Shackleton volunteered to tent with the most irritable and belligerent man in the group becoming his encourager and confidant. It was a culture of extreme discipline and hard work where the men, including Shackleton, would drag and carry their lifeboats, walk for miles every day, row against extreme conditions, and eat barely enough food to survive. This was their culture: optimism, sacrifice, hard work and comradery—and it is what enabled them to succeed.

Every organization has a culture. It is the personality of the group, the collective attitude, the group of norms of behavior and the underlying common values that keep those norms in place. Ravasi and Schultz state that organizational culture is a set of shared mental assumptions that guide action in organizations by defining appropriate behavior.[4] It is why, for example, when everyone at your job is supposed to arrive by 9:00 A.M., they actually arrive at either 8:45 A.M. or 9:15 A.M. It's not because the CEO decreed it, it's because of what has become the acceptable norm or tolerated taboo. It's why people wear jeans or khakis, show off their tattoos or keep them hidden, use racial slurs in the locker room, work extra hours or waste time at their computer. Culture is the accepted norm for behavior—despite what the written rules may be.

From where is culture derived? It usually comes from the leaders. People typically look to those in authority to disapprove or approve (even tacitly) certain behaviors. Leaders must understand that they teach people in their organization how to behave, how to treat one another and how to perform by what they allow, what they stop, and what they reinforce. The culture of the organization, shaped by the leader, will determine the credibility of the organization and, in fact, it's very survival.

A CULTURE OF COLLEGIALITY

Collegiality is the cooperative relationship of colleagues working together. More specifically, it is an organizational culture where collaboration and mutual submission exists between leaders. Again, collegiality is more than a relational dynamic—it is culture. It is when cooperation, collaboration, and accountability are underlying, shared values of the group's leaders. Even more, it is when these attributes become the behavioral norms and are consistently expressed within the organization's leadership structure.

The concept of a collegium first appeared in the Roman Republic. It was the practice of having at least two people, and always an even number, in each magistrate position of the Roman Senate. The reasons were to divide power and roles among a group of people, both to prevent the rise of another emperor and to ensure more productive magistrates.[5] From this ancient model of team leadership, we have developed modern day systems of checks and balances within civic, corporate, and even religious, organizations.

The trust of leadership is demonstrated where such collegiality exists in the culture of the entity. Rather than a bureaucracy where systems of control and management become necessary to regulate behavior, collegiality is a culture of interdependency among multiple group members, or leaders. No one person is supreme and above accountability, but each member is a vital component and equally empowered with the others. While each may have differing roles, responsibilities and levels of authority, these leaders pursue shared goals while working in a framework of trust, respect, and mutual submission.[6]

BUILDING A CULTURE OF COLLEGIALITY

Everywhere He went, He was leading, He was teaching, He was creating a new culture for those who would follow Him. When the children came to Jesus, He embraced them with tenderness. When the woman touched the hem of His garment, though unclean by her flow of blood, He accepted and healed her. When the demoniac of the Gadarenes, disheveled and filthy, chased after Him cursing and swearing, He set him free and put him in his right mind. When the prostitute washed His feet with her hair, when the adulteress was condemned before Him, He offered them forgiveness and restoration. He said love those that hate you, forgive those that malign you, give to those that ask you and pray for those that spitefully abuse you. And when He wrapped a towel around His waist, took a basin of water and a rag and knelt before His disciples and washed their feet one by one, He was showing them a new way to live and lead. It would be a culture where every person was valuable and no one, regardless of their title or position, could lord their authority over another. It was to be a culture of collegiality.

The gospel of John tells the story: "Jesus, knowing that the Father had given all things into His hands, and that He had come from God and was going to God, rose from supper and laid aside His garments, took a towel and girded Himself. After that, He poured water into a basin and began to wash the disciples' feet, and to wipe them with the towel with which He was girded. ...So when He had washed their feet, taken His garments, and sat down again, He said to them, 'Do you know what I have done to you? You call Me Teacher and Lord, and you say well, for so I am. If I then, your Lord and Teacher, have washed your feet, you also ought to wash one another's feet. For I have given you an example that you should do as I have done to you'" (John 13:3-15).

This is leadership according to Christ. Yes, one may have a title, and, yes, one may have authority and the right to command others, but never should that leader seek to elevate his worth over others or somehow imply that he is more important. Each of the disciples whose feet Jesus washed would become the future leaders of the church He was building. The message to them was clear: "If I then, your Lord and Teacher, have washed your feet, you also ought to wash one another's feet." Do not elevate yourselves over one another. Don't allow your egos to get in the way of serving together. Be a servant to one another. Value each other more than you value yourself. Defer to one another, support one another, trust one another, and serve one another. The culture of leadership in His Kingdom was to be a culture of collegiality. And when leaders serve as a collegium, the trust of leadership is secure.

So how does a leader promote collegiality? There are several elements that come together to demonstrate it.

MODESTY

In his landmark book, *Good to Great*, Jim Collins identifies Level 5 Leaders. He explains how these leaders are common to the most successful corporations in the U.S. Rather than being highly charismatic people who drive the organization by the force of their personality and seem to have all the answers, the Level 5 Leader is marked by modesty.

He writes, "Level 5 Leaders channel their ego needs away from themselves and into the larger goal of building a great company. It's not that Level 5 leaders have no ego or self-interest. Indeed, they are incredibly ambitious—but their ambition is first and foremost for the institution, not themselves."[7] These leaders may be strong and even forceful, but they are known more for their meekness.

While it may be true that many companies have been built into success by larger-than-life personalities who are able to motivate everyone by the force of their hard-driving, charismatic, "big-dog," extroversion, it is equally true that after these leaders left these companies, they sunk into decline. Organizations that are built on the power of the leader will usually die after that leader's power is gone.

By contrast, modesty in a leader is a model that has a longer term, and more sustainable success. Collins describes these leaders: "In contrast to the very I-centric style of the comparison leaders, we were struck by how the good-to-great leaders didn't talk about themselves. During interviews, they'd talk about the company and the contributions of other executives as long as we'd like but would deflect discussion about their own contributions. When pressed to talk about themselves, they'd say things like, 'I hope I'm not sounding like a big shot.' Or, 'If the board hadn't picked such great successors, you probably wouldn't be talking with me today.' Or, 'I don't think I can take much credit. We were blessed with marvelous people.'" Collins goes on, "It wasn't just false modesty. Those who worked with or wrote about the good-to-great leaders continually used words like 'quiet, humble, modest, reserved, shy, gracious, mild-mannered, self-effacing, understated' and so forth."[8]

The Bible calls it humility and it's the principle quality God requires of those in leadership. 1 Peter 5:6 says, "Therefore humble yourselves under the mighty hand of God, that He may exalt you in due time." James 4:10 tells us to "Humble yourselves in the sight of the Lord, and He will lift you up." In Isaiah 57:15 God speaks: "I dwell in the high and holy place with him who has a contrite and humble spirit to revive the spirit of the humble and to revive the heart of the contrite ones."

Leaders who are modest are able to regard the worth and value of others above their own. It's not that they are insecure or lack confidence. It's that they are self-aware. They realize their limitations and deficiencies and how they need the unique gifts of other leaders to compliment them. This is what Moses understood when he elevated a team of elders to help him judge the people (Exodus 18:24). It's what David realized when he surrounded himself with the Sons of Issachar who understood the times, to know what Israel should do (1 Chronicles 12:32). It's King Jehoshaphat knowing

The Trust of Leadership

he needed a prophet to help him understand the will of God (1 Kings 22:7).

John Maxwell calls it "The Law of the Lid." It is the limit of leadership potential that each leader has. By himself a leader can only go so high. But when he surrounds himself with others who have a higher "Leadership Lid," they will help him to go further.[9] This becomes clearer as we consider the next component of collegial leadership.

TEACHABILITY

Teachability is the capacity to "esteem others better than yourself" (Philippians 2:3) and "receive instruction" from them (Proverbs 10:17). The proud person believes that he has greater gifts, more experience and better skills than those around him and therefore has no need to listen to or esteem them. But the teachable spirit is willing to admit, "I don't have all the answers."

Most people see themselves as some kind of authority on almost anything. How often we hear, "If I were the leader…, if it was up to me…, if I was the pastor …this is what I would do." But rather than being wise in his own opinion (Romans 12:16, Proverbs 26:12), the teachable person readily admits, "I need guidance; I don't have all the answers; I need to be led." They are open and appreciative of others' suggestions.

This is a foundational element of trustworthy leadership. It means the leader must never be so arrogant and high minded that he is beyond correction. Trustworthy leaders are collegial. They can be instructed, they can be taught—they can be corrected or rebuked. And because they are teachable, they will be wise.

James 1:5 says, "If any of you lacks wisdom, let him ask of God, who gives to all liberally and without reproach, and it will be given to him." Indeed, God gives wisdom if we ask for it. But often that wisdom comes out of someone else's mouth. Question is, are we humble enough to receive it?

It is an issue of collegiality. Is there ample provision of wisdom, guidance, and knowledge around us, especially in the other leaders that surrounded us? On many occasions I have asked God for insight and guidance on issues. In answer to my prayer He always gives me the wisdom I seek by providing it through the deacons, elders, and other pastors around me. The key to receiving it is teachability. Will I be teachable enough to receive the guidance God is trying to supply me with through other leaders?

Leaders must realize that the leaders on their team are like glasses. Eyeglasses are what we need to give us 20/20 vision. As a leader, God will give me vision, but my vision isn't perfect. We see through a glass darkly (1 Corinthians 13:12). I have a sense of which direction God wants me to lead. It's a little blurry and I can't see everything clearly, but I'm pretty sure of where I need to go. Collegiality improves my vision. When I consult my leaders and remain teachable, it is like putting leadership glasses on. My deacons and board members help me discern better, they clarify and refine the vision, they give it more form and distinction. Through their input, if I remain teachable, I can know with greater accuracy what God is trying to do.

As noted in an earlier chapter, Rehoboam is an example of what happens to an unteachable leader who fails to use his leadership spectacles. God tried to give him sharper focus on where his policies would take him, but he refused the council of elders (1 Kings 12). He refused collegiality, and as result, lost his kingdom. Had he submitted to the godly counsel offered, his kingdom would have been preserved. This comes into sharper focus with the next attribute of collegial leadership.

SUBMISSION

2 Chronicles 25:16-21 describes King Uzziah's great success, how he prospered the nation and established Judah as a military superpower. However, when he became strong "...his heart was lifted up" and he believed himself superior to those around him, even the priests. He reasoned: "I am king. God has favored me

The Trust of Leadership

above all other men. Thousands of souls bow before me. Why must I defer to some cleric to offer incense for me? I can burn my own incense—I have a 'special' relationship with God and need not submit to a lowly priest." In the pride of his heart, he refused to be a collegial leader.

With this attitude, Uzziah entered the sanctuary and offered incense to God—a blatant violation of mosaic protocol. Immediately, the high priest along with eighty others confronted the king and said, "It is not for you, Uzziah, to burn incense to the Lord, but for the priests, the sons of Aaron, who are consecrated to burn incense. Get out of the sanctuary, for you have trespassed! You shall have no honor from the Lord God." As a result, God judged Uzziah by striking him with leprosy—a sign of spiritual uncleanness and public humiliation. King Uzziah, because he rejected correction, because he resisted instruction, remained leprous until the day of his death.

No matter how high in position a person may be, no matter how great their authority or position, no one is beyond needing counsel or even being corrected. Leaders, like anyone else, must know when to submit.

Let's be clear, submission is not agreement. Anyone can submit when he or she is in agreement with their leader. Uzziah would have easily obeyed the priest if he agreed with the priest; it was the priest's rebuke and contradiction that tested the sincerity of Uzziah's capacity for submission.

True submission is demonstrated, not in times of agreement, but in seasons of disagreement. In fact, there is no expression of submission without the context of disagreement. Without disagreement, submission is merely compliance. There is no need to restrain one's impulse or force one's obedience—one needs only to agree with that which he already views favorable.

On the contrary, it is one's ability to resist that surge of disagreement rising in one's heart—it is that discipline to quell an impulse of assertiveness against another's criticism, advice or counsel that proves true submission and the presence of real humility. Indeed, there are times when the leader must lead, but there are equally as many times when the leader must collaborate, cooperate, be teachable, submit, and create a collegial culture.

In doing so, he will promote a spirit of unity on his team and in the organization. This brings us to the next element of collegiality.

UNITY

Most leadership teams have an inclination toward either trust or suspicion. Boards that are unhealthy and dysfunctional act like watchdogs, making sure no one "gets away" with anything. As a result these teams are made up of adversarial relationships believing their role is to protect the organization from other inept or corrupt leaders.

Sadly, any organization rises or falls on the strength of the relationships that make it up—especially on the leadership team. Leadership teams that lack unity and collegiality are doomed to fail.

Absalom, the son of King David, had seized the throne. David was on the run. In his wisdom, the now fugitive king knew that if Absalom was to be defeated, his leadership team would need to be divided. So in 2 Samuel 15:34, he instructed his friend Hushai to serve as Absalom's counselor and undermine the credibility of Ahithophel's counsel, another of Absalom's advisors. Hushai did as David instructed and caused Absalom to reject Ahithophel's counsel. As a result, 2 Samuel 17:23 says Ahithophel "…put his household in order, hanged himself and died." This division in Absalom's leadership team was the beginning of his downfall.

In his book, *The Unity Factor*, Larry Osborne provides three ways leadership teams can improve their culture. Rather than remaining disconnected and suspicious of one another, very simple and practical steps can be taken to promote trust and respect and healthy collaboration.[10]

First, utilize the right meeting place. Sometimes, meeting in an office, sitting in metal chairs, or in a cold, cinderblock classroom only perpetuates a poor relational dynamic on the board. Location and atmosphere matters. Often these places keep things formal and stoic, cold, and clinical. What may help many teams transform this is meeting in a less formal, more comfortable location—like a home.

When people visit a home, they come with a different attitude. There is a friendly, welcoming tone that often puts people at ease. It sends the message, "You are welcome in my home, near my family, in my inner most place of safety—my home." People start to feel trusted, respected, even loved. Osborne explains it like this: "When we meet in an office or board room environment, we are surrounded by symbols of the corporate world, where confrontation and competition are expected. But when we meet in a home, the behavioral expectations are warmth, cooperation, and friendship."

Second, avoid placing business concerns above relationships. Look for ways to create a culture of fellowship and friendship outside of the board meetings. Take trips to special events together. Conduct a weekend retreat. Eat meals together, go fishing, paint someone's house. Take the time to invest in relationships and allow a spirit of togetherness to develop in the culture. This will cause you to laugh together, pray together, even cry together. Rather than only discussing financial statements and policy items, you'll be having deep, personal dialogues that bind people together at the heart.

These dynamics are an invaluable part of a healthy culture. You'll begin to see one another as people with cares and concerns. It has a "humanizing" effect which engenders vulnerability and trust and eventually respect.

A third element that is needed to build unity and collegiality is regular, consistent meetings. Rather than hastily planned, rushed meetings, so we can quickly end them and "get home to relax," we must realize that leadership meetings are crucial in developing what Peter Drucker called the "essential ingredient for teamwork: respect."[11] It is only through time together that leaders come to know each other well enough to have confidence in each other's ability to perform. It is by meeting together that we develop an appreciation for one another's competencies, motives and concerns.

MUTUAL ACCOUNTABILITY

Even the Apostle Peter needed accountability. In Galatians 2:11-14, Paul related the incident in which he "withstood him to his face" because he catered to the Jews and misrepresented the gospel to the Gentiles. It shows us that Paul, Peter, Barnabas and the rest of the apostles maintained a culture of collegiality between them. They understood that none of them were above correction and from time to time would need some accountability.

David Watson wrote, "Anything that is subject to human limitation or error requires the collegial presence of another person to ensure responsibility. It is a fact of life."[12] Human frailty demands our need for accountability. People are not always so upright that they just naturally do what they should. Structures will always be needed to ensure that people carry out their responsibilities. People fall short, they forget. They get sidetracked and lose interest. They slack off and just plain shirk their responsibilities. This is why accountability is needed.

A study conducted by McKinsey & Company examining organizational performance on an international basis revealed that a lack of accountability within the culture of an organization is the single greatest threat to achieving consistent levels of high performance. They analyzed revenue, growth, and profitability of global companies over a 10-year span and learned that only nine of the 1,077 companies examined (less than 1 percent) achieved measurable success. The one common flaw that each of the executives said they needed to improve: the lack of accountability among management and workers.[13]

Steven Covey said, "Accountability breeds responsibility." Being surrounded by people who challenge us to do better is a great asset. In fact, God often brings such people around us, not because we need to be saved from corruption, but because we need to be saved from mediocrity. They call us higher, they reject inferior performance, they force us to study deeper, work harder, and persevere longer. Those who have the benefit of such support are destined to succeed. This is how the Kingdom of God works. It favors the humble who submit to accountability and resists the proud who rejects the wisdom that can only come by submitting.

The following are seven practical means of ensuring a culture of accountability:

(1) Provide clear expectations of duties and tasks. People cannot be held accountable unless they know what is expected of them. Written job descriptions should be provided that outline requirements, responsibilities, and performance expectations.

(2) Offer regular feedback to those we are leading. Never underestimate how much subordinates need feedback from their leaders. This includes evaluations, directions, corrections, creative problem solving, and simply to know that the leader acknowledges them.

(3) Be quick to affirm those who do well. Leaders are quick to notice poor performance but often fail to acknowledge good performance. Offer praise for a job well done. Seek ways to acknowledge a person's achievement, especially in front of other team members or publically.

(4) Be willing to address the "brutal facts." In *Good to Great,* Jim Collins lists this as an essential duty of leadership. We must be willing to emphasize where we are falling short or failing to fulfill our vision. This helps to identify specific, measurable targets for improvement.

(5) Assign improvement metrics for those who fall short.

Provide practical, concrete areas that need to be improved. Identify how improvement will be measured. Be sure, however, to follow up and review progress as promised. This is where many leaders undermine their own credibility and the collegiality of the culture.

(6) Provide coaching when needed. Studies show that students need four positive comments to offset the impact of just one negative comment made by a teacher. The ratio increases to seven positive comments when a parent made the negative remark. This is similar to those we lead. Be sure to use the sandwich method: when criticizing performance, begin with a positive, affirming remark, followed by the criticism and then concluded with another positive. Criticism tastes much better when it's put in a sandwich.

(7) Offer other opportunities to serve. We don't call it being "fired." Instead, we are freeing people up to pursue other opportunities. Some people will simply not be capable of fulfilling the job and will need to be let go. Always do this with tenderness and fairness, but be forthright, truthful and transparent. Assume that people want to know where they failed and why they're being let go so they can make improvements.

FINAL THOUGHTS

Collegiality is the cooperative relationship of colleagues working together. It is an organizational culture where collaboration and mutual submission exists between leaders. Again, collegiality is more than a relational dynamic—it is culture. It is when cooperation, collaboration, and accountability are underlying, shared values of the group's leaders. Even more, it is when these attributes become the behavioral norms and are consistently expressed within the organization's leadership structure.

Leaders are responsible for culture. It is up to the leader to create a culture where modesty, teachability, submission, unity and accountability are norms for all—and preserve the trust of leadership.

The Trust of Leadership

The Trust of Leadership

A FINAL WORD

Character is not always enough.

Character is the outward demonstration of one's internalized moral code. It is an inner sense of right and wrong the drives one's decisions and determines his or her actions, reactions and inactions.

When it is said that a man or woman has character, it is implied that he or she has the resolve, the commitment to do what is right and ethical regardless of the risk, the cost involved or how inconvenient it may be. When it comes to trust in leadership, character is the most important quality a leader must have. It does not matter how gifted, anointed or strong a leader is, character is the essential foundation.

But character is not always enough.

David was a man after God's own heart (Acts 13:22). This is why God chose him. In 1 Samuel 16:7, He told the prophet Samuel, "Do not look at his appearance or at his physical stature…for the LORD does not see as man sees; for man looks at the outward appearance, but the LORD looks at the heart." Obviously, the Lord saw something pure and upright about David that qualified him to be king.

Unfortunately, David was still a man. As good as his character may have been, he was still a depraved, fallen creature. As such, he was subject to the corruption that often comes with authority unchecked.

As king, David was sovereign, so his actions were absolute and beyond question. No one dared challenge the king's opinion or contest his will. Whatever the king wanted, the king would get. Sadly, this power unchecked and absolute became the cause for two tragic failures both in his personal life and his leadership charge. The first was a scandalous affair with Bathsheba and the murder of her husband in 2 Samuel 11 and the second occurred when he numbered Israel to bring glory to himself in 1 Chronicles 21.

It's the "David Dilemma." Every person, regardless of how strong his or her character, WILL be promoted beyond what their character can support. It's the peril of our insidious, human nature. Jeremiah 17:9 says, "The heart is deceitful above all things, and desperately wicked." As good as one may be, if there are no restraints or restrictions upon him or her, if a person is free to act without any accountability or answerability, that person will be corrupted by his own depraved desires and driven to satisfy his own carnal interests. It is a sad fact of human nature, authority without accountability corrupts.

The failures of King David, the man after God's own heart, demonstrate why leaders, even good leaders, need structures of accountability. Transparency, reportability, fiduciary, humility, collegiality all work together to provide the leader with the structures needed to maintain his integrity—and his credibility.

Leadership without accountability is leadership without credibility. Structures of accountability are not meant to hinder leaders or hold them back, they are meant to empower leaders and propel them forward. They are guardrails keeping leaders centered and secure. Followers, investors, employees who see leaders with such guardrails will be more inclined to trust them and follow wherever they may lead.

Every leader would do well to make accountability a priority. Success is great, but without accountability it will bring a downfall.

May we conclude by sharing the following prayer:

THE LEADER'S PRAYER

"Heavenly Father, I thank you for the call upon my life to lead. I want to achieve what You call me to achieve. I want to build what You call me to build. But first I want to be a person of character—a leader who is trustworthy.

"Heavenly Father, I recognize that I am but flesh and that my heart is deceitful above all things and desperately wicked. Therefore I ask You to surround me with capable men and women who can strengthen my character by providing accountability.

"Heavenly Father, help me to establish checks and balances in my life to protect me from myself. Help me to submit to accountability, reportability, transparency, fiduciarity, humility and collegiality to strengthen my credibility.

"Heavenly Father, this is my prayer. Do not allow me to be promoted beyond what my character can support. Prevent me from being enlarged beyond what my integrity can bare. Surround me with healthy structures of accountability that can sustain my promotion and protect my character."

The Trust of Leadership

ENDNOTES

Introduction
1. See article at http://www.attask.com/newsletters/do-you-trust-your-work-like-the-ancient-roman-engineers
2. See article at: http://www.whitehouse.gov/the-press-office/remarks-president-ghanaian-parliament
3. See article at: http://www.gallup.com/poll/1654/honesty-ethics-professions.aspx
4. See article at http://news.bbc.co.uk/go/pr/fr/-/2/hi/africa/6294666.stm
5. See article at http://news.bbc.co.uk/go/pr/fr/-/2/hi/africa/5083534.stm
6. Stephen M. R. Covey; *The Speed of Trust: The One Thing That Changes Everything*, (Free Press, New York, 2006)

Chapter One
1. Guy I. Seidman; *The Origins of Accountability; Everything I know about the Sovereigns' Immunity, I learn from King Henry III*; (Saint Louis University Law Journal, Vol. 49, No. 2, Winter 2004/2005)
2. See article at: http://www.emersonkent.com/historic_documents/magna_carta_1215.htm
3. Ronald Enroth; *Churches That Abuse* (Grand Rapids: Zondervan, 1992) pg. 189

Chapter Two
1. See article at: http://www.transparency.org/whatwedo/activity/curbing_corruption_in_public_procurement
2. Robert Eccles, *The ValueReporting Revolution* (PriceWaterhouseCoopers LLP, Canada, 2001)
3. See article at: http://www.cbsnews.com/news/senate-panel-probes-6-top-televangelists/
4. See article at: http://www.npr.org/2014/04/02/298373994/onscreen-but-out-of-sight-tv-preachers-avoid-tax-scrutiny
5. See article at: http://www.icmpa.umd.edu/pages/studies/transparency/main.html

Chapter Three
1. See article at: http://www.christianitytoday.com/gleanings/2014/february/founder-of-worlds-largest-megachurch-convicted-cho-yoido.html
2. See article at: http://english.hani.co.kr/arti/english_edition/e_national/611326.htmlhttp://english.hani.co.kr/arti/english_edition/e_national/611326.html
3. See article at http://english.hani.co.kr/arti/english_edition/e_national/611326.htmlhttp://english.hani.co.kr/arti/english_edition/e_national/611326.html
4. See article at http://www.gospelherald.com/articles/50481/20140221/full-gospel-church-founder-david-yonggi-cho-found-guilty-of-breach-of-trust-corruption.htm
5. See article at: http://www.koreaherald.com/view.php?ud=20120528000348&mod=skb
6. See article at: http://www.gasb.org/plain-language_documents/ConceptSt4_PLA.pdf

7. See article at: http://www.ecfa.org/Content/Comment3
8. See article at: https://www.barna.org/donorscause-articles/571-the-economy-continues-to-squeeze-americans-charitable-giving
9. See article at: https://www.barna.org/barna-update/article/5-barna-update/121-tithing-down-62-in-the-past-year#.U3FC_vldX3Y

Chapter Four
1. Heritage Village Church and Missionary Fellowship, Inc. 92 B.R. 1000 (D.S.C. 1988)
2. Peifer, Justice Paul E. (April 12, 2000). *Jim Bakker's Federal Court Appeal.* Supreme Court of Ohio website.
3. Ibid
4. Ibid
5. Michael J. Anthony; *The Effective Church Board* (Baker Books, Grand Rapids, Michigan, 1993) pg. 47
6. See article at: http://www.ecologia.org/isosr/fiduciarity.html
7. Marion R. Fremont-Smith, Andras Kosaras; Wrongdoing *by Officers and Directors of Charities* (The Hauser Center for Nonprofit Organizations, The Kennedy School of Government Harvard University; September 2003, Working Paper No. 20)
8. Richard R. Hammer; *Pastor, Church & Law, Volume 2* (Christianity Today International, Carol Stream Il. 2008) pgs. 150-184
9. See article at: http://www.ecfa.org/Content/Comment3
10. Trethewey v. Green River gorge, 136 P.2d 999, 1012 (Wash. 1943)

Chapter Five
1. Martin Meredith, *The Fate of Africa* (Public Affairs NY) pg. 220
2. Steve H, Hanke; Alex KF Kwok (Spring–Summer 2009). *On the Measurement of Zimbabwe's Hyperinflation* (PDF). The Cato Journal.
3. See article at: http://www.newzimbabwe.com/pages/palace.html
4. Martin Meredith, *The Fate of Africa* (Public Affairs NY) pg. 221
5. Nelson Mandela's statement at the opening of the defense case in the Rivonia Trial (Pretoria Supreme Court, April 20, 1964
6. Robert Calderisi, *The Trouble with Africa* (Palgrave MacMillian NY) pg. 66
7. See article at: http://www.ravenhill.org/dayincourt.htm
8. Robert Greenleaf; *The Servant as Leader* (The Robert K. Greenleaf Center; Westfield In. 1970)

Chapter Six
1. Browning, B. W. (2007). Leadership in desperate times: An analysis of "Endurance: Shackleton's Incredible Voyage" through the lens of leadership theory. *Advances in Developing Human Resources, 9,* 183-198.
2. Lansing, A. (2002). *Endurance: Shackleton's incredible voyage.* New York: Carroll & Graf.
3. http://www.psychologytoday.com/blog/the-good-life/201101/leading-in-trying-times-the-case-ernest-shackleton
4. Ravasi, D., Schultz, M. (2006), "Responding to organizational identity threats: exploring the role of organizational culture", *Academy of Management Journal,* Vol.49, No.3, pp. 433–458
5. See article at: http://en.wikipedia.org/wiki/Collegiality
6. See article at: http://www.thefreedictionary.com/collegium
7. Jim Collins; *Good to Great* (Harper Collins, NY) pg. 21

8. Ibid. pg. 27
9. John C. Maxwell; *The 21 Irrefutable Laws of Leadership* (Maxwell Motivation, Georgia) pg. 1
10. Larry Osborne; *The Unity Factor* (Owl's Nest; Vista, California, 1989) pgs. 23-28.
11. Peter Drucker; *Baseball, Business & Teamwork* (Boardroom Reports; June 15, 1986), pg. 9
12. David Watson; *Covenant Discipleship* (Nashville: Discipleship Resources, 1996), pg. 17.
13. Greg Bustin; *Accountability: The Key to Driving a High-Performance Culture* (McGraw Hill Education; New York, 2014) pg. xii

About the Author

Gregg T. Johnson is Senior Pastor of The Mission Church in New York, USA. He is ordained with The Assemblies of God and serves as a New York District Presbyter overseeing the Hudson Valley Section in New York. He and his wife Laura raised four sons, one daughter and have two grandsons.

Pastor Gregg is also founder and keynote speaker of Global Leadership Training, an international equipping ministry that provides leadership training conferences to pastors and church leaders in developing nations. These conferences provide practical teaching on character development, leadership ethics, and ministry management. Thousands of leaders have been enriched by Global Leadership Training and Pastor Gregg's ministry throughout Africa, India, Canada, and the U.S.

Gregg Johnson has authored six books covering various topics of leadership and ministry:

The Character of Leadership

Raising the Standard of Leadership

Ethics for Church Leaders

Crises, Conflict and Change

How the Mighty Have Fallen

The Trust of Leadership

He also publishes *Leadership Teaching Magazine*, a 24 page online magazine which addresses important topics on leadership and ministry and is provided to thousands of pastors throughout the world. For more information contact:

The Mission Church
4101 Rt. 52 Holmes, NY 12531

Or visit him online at
www.GreggTJohnson.com